The Price of Defeat: The History of British Operation Technology, and Equipment from Germany to Brita

By Charles River Editors

A picture of Allied soldiers inspecting the German experimental nuclear pile at Haigerloch

About Charles River Editors

Charles River Editors provides superior editing and original writing services across the digital publishing industry, with the expertise to create digital content for publishers across a vast range of subject matter. In addition to providing original digital content for third party publishers, we also republish civilization's greatest literary works, bringing them to new generations of readers via ebooks.

Sign up here to receive updates about free books as we publish them, and visit Our Kindle Author Page to browse today's free promotions and our most recently published Kindle titles.

Introduction

Reparations and reconstruction are once again in the news as conflicts in Afghanistan, Iraq, Syria and the Islamic State approach a conclusion. Territorial claims, for example Kurdistan, need to be settled, and victims are calling for justice, especially where war crimes are alleged. Refugees need to be resettled and infrastructure restored while the victors seek to learn military lessons and take whatever economic and political advantage they can. These are the latest manifestations of a public debate about how to "win the peace" which began with the unsatisfactory Versailles Conference in 1919 and contributed to the very different responses by the Allies after the defeat of Germany in 1945.

After the last shots of World War II were fired and the process of rebuilding Germany and Europe began, the Western Allies and the Soviet Union each tried to obtain the services of the Third Reich's leading scientists, especially those involved in rocketry, missile technology, and aerospace research. Naturally, this was a delicate affair due to the fact many of the German scientists were not only active Nazis but had helped the Nazi war machine terrorize the world. At the same time, by the late war period, the Anglo-American Allies formed a clear picture of the Soviet state. Though forced to ally with the USSR's dictator, the West came to understand Communist Russia represented yet another hungry totalitarian power, and thus a very real threat to an independent Europe. British Prime Minister Winston Churchill realized the menacing character of the Soviets from the Katyn Forest Massacre of Polish army officers, if not before, while the Americans only gradually shed a naïve assumption of continued Russian friendliness after the war.

For their part, the Soviets retained ruthless imperial ambitions which manifested in various ways. They allied with Hitler for a time in 1939 to 1941, planning to divide Eastern Europe between their two expansionist states. They devastated the Ukrainian population with the Holomodor, an engineered, genocidal famine which claimed perhaps 3 million victims. The Soviet refusal to evacuate Eastern Europe following the war, instead retaining many formerly democratic countries as vassal states, spoke volumes about their intentions.

Both the Western Allies and the Soviets knew of Adolf Hitler's V-2 rocket program, the forerunner of ballistic missiles and the space race. Each recognized the immense strategic value of these technologies and wished to secure their benefits for themselves. As the Soviets contemplated additional expansion following the "Great Patriotic War" and the U.S. military came to understand the putative allies of today would emerge as the enemies of tomorrow, the men possessing knowledge of the V-2 rockets and other Third Reich military technology programs became seen as crucial pieces in the incipient NATO versus Warsaw Pact standoff.

The result was the American-led "Operation Paperclip" on the Western side, which resulted in German scientists putting their expertise at the disposal of the U.S. and other NATO members. Operation Paperclip aimed not only to obtain the benefits of German scientific advances for the

United States but also to deny them to the potentially hostile Soviets, as General Leslie Groves enunciated: "Heisenberg was one of the world's leading physicists, and, at the time of the German break-up, he was worth more to us than *ten divisions* of Germans. Had he fallen into the Russian hands, he would have proven invaluable to them (Naimark, 1995, 207).

The Western approach, however self-interested, typically met with voluntary compliance on the German scientists' parts. In contrast, the Soviet answer to Paperclip, Operation Osoaviakhim, used the implied threat of imprisonment, torture, and death, the characteristic tools of Stalinist Russia, to coerce assistance from German scientists and engineers following the war. These men yielded rich dividends to the Soviet state in terms of achieving at least temporary technical parity with the USSR's western rivals.

To say these operations had a profound impact on the Cold War and American history would be an understatement. The most well-known example of Operation Paperclip's "success" was Wernher von Braun, who was once a member of a branch of the SS involved in the Holocaust before becoming known as the "father of rocket science" and fascinating the world with visions of winged rockets and space stations as a "new" Manhattan Project, one that NASA would eventually adopt. In addition to the weaponization of ballistic missiles that progressed throughout the Cold War, von Braun's expertise was used for America's most historic space missions. While NASA developed rockets capable of first launching a spacecraft into Earth's orbit, and then launching it toward the Moon, the Soviets struggled throughout the 1960s to design rockets up to the task. Thanks to von Braun, NASA got it right with the Saturn V rocket, which to this day remains the most powerful launching rocket NASA ever used.

There is an enormous amount of documentation about the American efforts, particularly Operation Paperclip and its ultimate outcomes, yet the parallel programs involving the transfer of personnel, intellectual property (IP), and equipment to the UK have attracted limited academic study and are almost forgotten by the general public. A pioneering article by John Farquharson in 1997 assessed the extent and nature of British transfers, but research into the military and civilian units that carried out the transfers had to wait until the partial declassification of official files in 2006. This was followed by the publication of sensationalist and generalized allegations of unethical practices in the mass media, which prompted personal memoirs in book form from Michael Howard (2010) and in the popular press.

The first full length, academic book by Sean Longden (2009), based on extensive use of official archives and the personal memoirs of many more veterans, showed how British policy evolved amidst a rapidly changing geopolitical context. The most recent work by Charlie Hall (2019) is the most academic treatment of the topic so far and focuses more deeply on that geopolitical context, especially the emerging Cold War, and it also made use of many more archival sources. Hall also emphasized the importance of what he terms "exploitation" of equipment, IP, and personnel, and the work demonstrated how the emphasis gradually shifted towards the latter.

However, Hall never justified his choice of the term exploitation. In business it means maximizing the value of resources but in the social sciences it sometimes has connotations of one-sided abuse of power. Significantly, Hall ignored the positive inputs the British made to the reconstruction of Germany, averting famine in the winter of 1945 and 1946 and rebuilding infrastructure.

The Price of Defeat: The History of British Operations to Transfer Personnel, Technology, and Equipment from Germany to Britain after World War II examines the Nazis' technologies and personnel, and the various efforts by the British to access them as the war was coming to a close.

Nazi Technologies Before and During the War

Though extremely different men in most ways, British Prime Minister Winston Churchill and Third Reich Fuhrer Adolf Hitler shared a passion for science, technology, and (sometimes impractical) "wonder weapons." In some cases, this fixation paid off handsomely, as in the case of British centrimetric radar, a compact, powerful radar type that enabled fitment to individual aircraft and contributed to the defeat of German U-boats.

Germany's science obviously failed to snatch victory from the jaws of defeat as Hitler fondly imagined it might. Nevertheless, the Germans made several crucial advances, including the first functional jet fighter aircraft, infrared sights for sniper rifles, plans for a "flying wing" style aircraft, nuclear bomb research, and V-1 and V-2 rocket technology.

Though some of Hitler's weapon programs inflicted damage on the Allies, most proved counterproductive from the Third Reich's point of view. They used up vast quantities of money, material, and know-how which otherwise could have produced large numbers of ordinary but effective aircraft or vehicles. In effect, Germany's experimental science programs hindered its war effort and produced advances whose benefits accrued mostly to its enemies, both eastern and western. The V-2 rocket even caused problems for the German food supply, since each rocket's fuel required the rendering of 30 tons of potatoes to produce sufficient alcohol.

Most spectacularly, the Germans laid the groundwork for the era of ballistic missiles to follow with the "Vengeance Weapons" program. The advent of relatively advanced liquid and solid fuels for rocket weapons made them viable again after a period during which rifled artillery overshadowed them. An additional factor creating German interest in military rockets came from their complete omission among the restrictions placed on Germany's army by the Treaty of Versailles at the end of World War I. This major loophole led the Germans to hope improved rocketry could replace artillery, which the Treaty nearly banned.

A V-2 rocket

The Germans also felt considerable popular enthusiasm for spaceflight, reinforced by the well-received 1929 science fiction film *Woman in the Moon*, produced by Fritz Lang. Max Valier, an Austrian author, also promoted spaceflight, interplanetary exploration, and spread knowledge of the potential offered by liquid-fuel rockets to an intrigued public. Thus, rocket science achieved both popular cachet and official backing in 1920s to 1930s Germany.

By contrast, Russian and American rocket scientists failed to drum up support despite their insights and advances. Robert Goddard launched the first-ever liquid-fuel rocket in 1926 but met only mockery and scorn from the press, which then ignored him. Konstantin Tsiolkovsky wrote extensively on the subject but achieved no acclaim. Ironically, both the Americans and Russians – who ignored their own rocket scientists earlier – embraced the German fad after exposure to Third Reich science in World War II.

Goddard

German rocketry continued to develop in the 1930s, largely driven by the inexorable enthusiasm of Hermann Oberth, who recruited the young Freiherr (baron) Wernher von Braun, a fellow enthusiast of the possibilities of spaceflight. An eccentric but highly motivated congeries of young engineers, scientists, and workmen came together to found the "Raketenflugplatz," or "Rocket Flying Plaza," the first construction and testing ground for modern rockets in the world. Eventually, von Braun's combination of easy, friendly personal charm and family clout won the rocketry enthusiasts Army backing and funding, albeit at the cost of secrecy and outside control.

Oberth

Von Braun

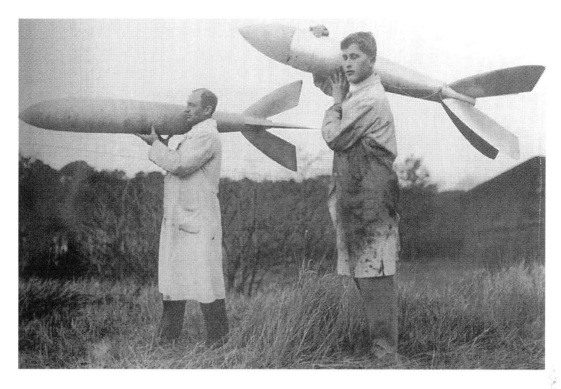

Rockets at the Raketenflugplatz

While most of the men felt patriotic and even nationalistic attachment to Germany, their motives centered mostly on being able to finally obtain the funding needed to create the rockets all of them dreamed of, as von Braun once explained: "There has been a lot of talk that the Raketenflugplatz finally 'sold out to the Nazis.' In 1932, however, when the die was cast, the Nazis were not yet in power, and to all of us Hitler was just another mountebank on the political stage. Our feelings toward the Army resembled those of the early aviation pioneers [...] The issue in these discussions was merely how the golden cow could be milked most successfully." (Neufeld, 1995, 26).

The "golden cow" gave much more "milk" following the rise of the Nazis to power several years later. While the army of the Weimar Republic wanted to restore German strength in case of an eventual war, Hitler and the other National Socialist leaders wanted swift revenge and immediate territorial aggrandizement. The strengthening of the Soviet Union during the 1930s also provided impetus to rearmament.

Before the Second World War, military conflicts were fought under orthodox conditions, usually termed "conventional warfare," but several innovations had significantly changed combat, leading inextricably to the race for a nuclear weapon in the 1930s and 1940s. Conflicts had been fought by armies on horseback with guns of varying sophistication since the 16th century, but mechanized warfare and machine guns changed this calculus and set the stage for future combat by the end of World War I. Other sinister changes entered the fray during this conflict, such as chemical weapons like chlorine and mustard gas.

The total warfare brought about by World War I and ensuing wars like the Spanish Civil War made the quest for nuclear weapons somewhat necessary, and it would happen to coincide with the Nazis' rise to power in Germany. Only founded in 1871, the German *Reich* (Empire) unified the German-speaking states that mostly constituted the long-lived Holy Roman Empire, but it was dominated by Prussia, one of Europe's foremost military powers. Prussia had a long-standing military tradition that pervaded every strata of society, and it infused the German *Reich* after 1871. Simultaneously, the unified Germany's economy grew very quickly, seeking new markets and new territory.

After losing World War I, Germany was stripped of 10% of its territory and most of its military might, and it was forced to pay huge financial sums as reparations. The Weimar Republic, the democratic state that followed the war, was allowed a standing army of only 100,000 troops (it had previously 3.8 million men under arms) and a navy of only six ships. Germany was prohibited from having an air force and could not station any soldiers in the Rhineland region bordering France, Belgium, and the Netherlands.

All of these conditions were fiercely opposed by the majority of the German population, many of whom either did not believe or failed to accept that Germany had lost the war. It was only the threat of invasion that forced German politicians to sign the 1918 armistice to end the war and the subsequent 1919 Treaty of Versailles. Nevertheless, it was an unstated objective of Weimar governments to overturn many of Versailles' conditions or at least soften them, so when the Nazis came to power in January 1933, partly as a result of the desperation inflicted upon the German population after 1919, Hitler's regime essentially ignored the Treaty's military commitments.

One of the successes of the pre-war Nazi state was that it operated a "war economy," providing jobs and wages after the deprivation of the early 1930s, and in so doing the Nazis rapidly rearmed the country's military forces. In 1935, Hitler gave his trusted lieutenant Hermann Göring the task of creating a German air force, or Luftwaffe. The Rhineland was also reoccupied as the Nazis built up a military machine that could reclaim lost territories and, if necessary, defeat other European powers in acquiring new ones. Hitler's plans went well beyond Germany's pre-World World I strength to achieve overwhelming superiority, and creating a super weapon such as a nuclear bomb could help achieve the goal, which was one of the reasons it was so appealing to Hitler and his subordinates.

The scientific breakthroughs of the first decades of the 20th century would play a vital role. German physicist Otto Hahn, with the assistance of his research partner Fritz Strassmann and the theoretical expertise of Hahn's niece Lise Meitner, split the atom for the first time in history on December 17, 1938 in Berlin. A uranium isotope - Uranium 235 - was bombarded by neutrons, causing it to become highly unstable. Temporarily becoming a separate version of the isotope, it released a large amount of energy when split, and the reaction became known as nuclear fission.

By then, Meitner had fled the Nazis' persecution of Jews, making her one of countless German scientists the Nazis ultimately failed to fully utilize due to their Jewishness.

Hahn

Meitner

A number of other prominent scientists went into exile after the Nazis came to power in 1933, and the loss of so many bright minds has led historians to the conclusion that the exodus could have made the difference between Germany winning the race for a nuclear bomb. That most of the scientists were Jewish was further proof that in addition to being dogmatically racist, the Nazis were also incompetent and self-defeating.

Germany had a scarcity of top-level scientists after the First World War for the simple reason that many had to fight in the conflict, and this was exacerbated in the 1930s when many of the country's most capable researchers fled Nazi Germany. An early Nazi-era law was passed essentially expelling Jewish academics from German universities, and many of these academics left the country as a result.

The impact on the physics community was particularly pronounced. It is estimated that around half of all German physicists cited in academic literature were forced out of Germany, and 11 of these physicists had won or would win the Nobel Prize. It is astonishing that an advanced country like Germany would participate in such an act of intellectual self-harm, but the trend was only made worse by the burgeoning *Deutsche Physik* (German Physics) movement, which combined nationalism and physics in a feeble attempt to provide intellectual support for the regime. *Deutsche Physik* members denounced "Jewish Physics" and recruited a large number of

German scientists who became increasingly concerned that their careers could be over unless they supported the movement, or worse.

Many of Germany's scientists were unsympathetic to the Nazis but made enough compromises to continue to work, including Hahn.[1] Meitner, who was from a Jewish family but had converted to Christianity, was a critic of the Nazi authorities but believed her Austrian passport gave her some degree of protection should there be a severe crackdown. After the Anschluss with Austria, Meitner was spirited out of Germany in July 1938, into the Netherlands and then to Sweden.[2] Meitner continued her work, including in Copenhagen with Niels Bohr, and she continued to correspond with Hahn, ultimately providing the intellectual theory and explanation for the fission experiment he carried out with Strassmann in late 1938. As such, Meitner could be considered a cofounder of nuclear fission along with Hahn, although only the latter received a Nobel Prize for his efforts.

Among the scientists who left Nazi Germany, the most famous was Albert Einstein, but there were other important ones like Fritz Haber, Max Born and Felix Bloch. Einstein had been awarded the Nobel Prize in 1921 at the age of 42 for his work on quantum theory, including his famous theory of relativity and the equation $E = mc^2$. Away in the United States when Hitler became Chancellor of Germany in January 1933, Einstein decided not to return due to his Jewish heritage, ultimately becoming an American citizen in 1940. Though he was considered a pacifist, Einstein nevertheless warned the American administration that the Hitler regime was seeking to develop a nuclear bomb.

Max Born, who worked at Göttingen with physicist Werner Heisenberg, taught, supervised or collaborated with eight researchers who subsequently worked on the United States' Manhattan Project, including Robert Oppenheimer and Edward Teller. It has been debated as to whether these scientists in and of themselves made the crucial difference between the American and German efforts to create a bomb because the Americans dedicated far greater personnel and resources to their Manhattan Project than the Germans did with their *Uranprojekt*. Regardless, it does seem indicative of the Nazi approach - blind ideology combined with malice - that they would force out some of the world's most talented scientists, only to have those scientists prove instrumental in developing the weapon they themselves failed to build.

The Nazis dominated Europe until June 1944, and during that time, Germany had access to every resource available, including slave labor. The *Uranprojekt* scientists worked on the nuclear project under the auspices of the HWA until 1942, when the program was effectively downgraded due to its lack of success.

---

[1] Jeremy Bernstein, *Plutonium: A History of the World's Most Dangerous Element*, (University of NSW Press, 2009), p. 43.
[2] Jeremy Bernstein, *Plutonium: A History of the World's Most Dangerous Element*, (University of NSW Press, 2009), p. 47.

There are a number of theories as to why the Nazi scientists failed to develop an atomic bomb. As discussed earlier, most of Germany's most able scientists fled the country during the 1930s. Furthermore, some believe that scientists who subsequently claimed to be unsympathetic to the Nazi cause, such as Heisenberg, impeded the project from within. Perhaps most importantly, the technology was insufficiently understood, and the Nazis failed to dedicate enough resources and funding to the project, particularly when compared to the huge sums spent on the American Manhattan Project.

Nonetheless, the *Uranprojekt* made some progress towards a weapon in the war's final years, even if it proved ultimately unsuccessful. It has been suggested that some, such as Carl Friedrich von Weizsäcker, hoped that success in this area would lead to political influence. In 1941, he drafted and revised an application for a patent, "Technical extraction of energy, production of neutrons, and manufacture of new elements by the fission of uranium or related heavier elements," setting out a process that would use neutrons to generate energy and an explosion.[3] In these documents, Weizsäcker, on behalf of the Kaiser Wilhelm Institute, also cited the importance of substance "94."

Weizsäcker, along with Heisenberg, also visited Denmark twice in 1941 to see Niels Bohr. The meetings took place in March and September, and they later became dramatized as the subject of a theatre play, *Copenhagen*, first performed in the 1990s.[4] There has been speculation about the contents of the meeting between Heisenberg and Bohr in particular, which took place when Nazi influence and power was probably at its zenith. Historians have speculated that Heisenberg sought Bohr's council regarding building a nuclear bomb. For his part, however, Bohr appeared upset by the contents of the meeting and did not want to play any role in helping the Nazis achieve their objective of a nuclear weapon.[5] The *Uranprojekt* itself lost momentum shortly afterwards as resources from across Germany were sucked into the increasingly fraught war effort.

Historians widely agree that Hitler and his regime made a series of strategic errors during 1941 and 1942 that ultimately made Germany's defeat more likely. Above all, the decision to attack the Soviet Union in 1941 was a major blunder. After initial success, mostly explained by the surprise element of "Operation Barbarossa," the Wehrmacht became embroiled in a brutal conflict they could not win. When the tide turned after the battles of 1942, the Nazis were on the road to defeat. Similarly, Hitler declared war on the United States after Japan's attack on Pearl Harbor in December 1941. This aligned the Soviet Union, United States and Britain all against Germany. It also meant that the Americans accelerated their own nuclear program, the Manhattan Project.[6]

---

[3] Rainer Karlsch and Mark Walker, "New Light on Hitler's Bomb", *Physics World*, 1 June 2005, https://physicsworld.com/a/new-light-on-hitlers-bomb/, [accessed 5 June 2019]

[4] Michael Frayn, *Copenhagen*, play first performed at the National Theatre, London, 1998.

[5] "The Bohr-Heisenberg Meeting", American Institute of Physics, https://history.aip.org/exhibits/heisenberg/bohr-heisenberg-meeting.htm, [accessed 7 June 2019]

In 1943, the Nazis were also forced out of North Africa by the Allies, who then turned to plans to attack German positions in occupied France and through Mussolini's Italy. Even as the Allies determined that they could not invade France until June 1944, leaders remained acutely aware that a new weapon would change the calculus of the conflict. The British had undergone almost daily bombardment from the *Luftwaffe* after the fall of France in June 1940. The Nazis targeted civilian centers, such as London, as well as industrial cities producing arms. Any Nazi nuclear weapon or other new weapon of mass destruction would likely be used on Britain. Churchill even made plans for the top secret "Operation Peppermint," the preparation of London for a nuclear attack.[7] Churchill was anxious that these remain secret so as not to lower the morale of the general population.

As a means of reducing the likelihood that Germany would develop a nuclear weapon, Churchill encouraged sabotage operations on German nuclear facilities. That said, accurate information has not been able to clarify the Nazis' nuclear strategy. Recent work suggests the Nazis were striving to construct a bomb until the end of the war in 1945, but others suggest that Hitler essentially downgraded the status of the *Uranprojekt* at the beginning of 1942. Certainly, the latter has some credence insofar as the project was taken out of the supervision of the HWA and army oversight and instead handed over to the Reich Research Council. The military still had a keen interest in the status of the project, but with scientists being withdrawn from the research, it does appear that the Nazis were unconvinced of the viability of a nuclear weapon.[8] Some of the *Uranprojekt* physicists were even drafted to fight on the front against the Soviet Union, reflecting the notion that the removal of resources from the nuclear weapons program most likely came about because of the war's deteriorating status.

Life under Nazi rule was grim, and the German occupiers treated the people they ruled over in Europe with harsh methods, draconian violence, and overwhelming suppression. By the middle of the war, the Nazis were sending Jews from across the continent to death camps, and a general crackdown increased in these years, trying to stamp out any dissent. In Denmark, the population had been mostly cowed during the first years of Nazi occupation, but this changed in 1942 following German defeats at Stalingrad and El-Alamein, which appeared to give some Danes hope the occupation might weaken. Strikes and disturbances increased in Denmark in 1943, and the Danish government was considered to be unreliable enough that the Nazis imposed martial law in August 1943.

Resistance groups operated across Europe, and a Danish resistance organization - the Danish

---

[6] Mary H. Williams, "Chronology 1941–1945", (Washington, D.C.: Office of the Chief of Military History, Department of the Army, 1960), pp. 3-4.

[7] Damien Lewis, "The Third Reich's nuclear program: Churchill's greatest wartime fear", *History Extra,* 22 March 2018, https://www.historyextra.com/period/second-world-war/the-third-reichs-nuclear-program-churchills-greatest-wartime-fear/, [accessed 3 June 2019]

[8] Mark Walker, *German National Socialism and the Quest for Nuclear Power 1939–1949* (Cambridge University Press, 1993), p. 52.

Freedom Council - formed and committed some acts of sabotage against the Nazis. This was the backdrop to Niels Bohr fleeing Denmark in 1943. Bohr had become aware that he was about to be arrested by the Nazis due to his mother being Jewish. Along with his family, Bohr was taken by the Danish Resistance to Sweden and then on to Scotland. The British knew the value of a renowned scientist such as Bohr and kept his arrival secret. They even had Bohr work with the British nuclear weapons team. He was then transported to the United States in late 1943, also covertly, where he met his old colleague Einstein in Princeton. Bohr visited Los Alamos in New Mexico more than once, where the Manhattan Project was based, and although he later claimed he was not involved in the nuclear weapons program, lead physicist Robert Oppenheimer claimed Bohr was like a "father figure" to the other scientists.[9]

Bohr, of course, had been close to Heisenberg, and he was apparently livid that his old colleague was working on the Nazi *Uranprojekt*. Heisenberg, however, was undeterred and continued his own theoretical work. He was appointed chair of theoretical physics at Berlin's main university in 1943, lectured in Switzerland, and visited Poland and Denmark.

During his visit to Switzerland, Heisenberg was almost caught up in an assassination attempt that can only be described as coming straight from a spy novel. The American Office of Strategic Services (OSS), the forerunner to the Central Intelligence Agency (CIA), had dispatched a number of agents to Europe to monitor Nazi and Italian attempts to develop new weapons as part of its "Project Larson." The project, similar to the "Alsos Mission," also focused on German scientists working on the Nazi weapons programs.

Project Larson had a particular interest in the activities of Heisenberg and Weizsäcker. One of the OSS' agents working on Project Larson was Major League Baseball player Morris "Moe" Berg, who was sent to Zürich, Switzerland to attend Heisenberg's lecture there in 1944. Details later emerged that Berg's orders were to shoot Heisenberg dead if he revealed anything that suggested the Nazis were close to developing a nuclear weapon.[10] In the end, Berg decided that nothing Heisenberg said during the lecture suggested the Nazis were close to completing an atomic bomb. It was further evidence that the Allies were highly concerned that Hitler may be close to a nuclear weapon.

These fears had been heightened by the use of other weapons as part of the Nazi's "V" weapons program. Eventually, the Third Reich's leaders chose the island of Usedom as the site for their rocket program. This elongated island lies just off the Pomeranian coast in the Baltic Sea, separated from the mainland by several lagoons. With beaches and the sunniest climate of any Baltic island, Usedom represented a popular tourist resort from the 19th century through the early 21st century.

---

[9] Abraham Pais, *Niels Bohr's Times, In Physics, Philosophy and Polity* (Oxford: Clarendon Press, 1991), p. 497.

[10] William Tobey, "Nuclear Scientists as Assassination Targets", *Bulletin of the Atomic Scientists*, 68: 1 (January 2012, pp. 61–69)

The Germans built their rocket facility at Peenemünde, at the mouth of the Peene River, where King Gustavus II Adolphus, the so-called "Lion from Midnight," and his Swedish army landed during the Thirty Years War. The coastal location enabled rocket tests without fear of hitting inhabited land, with ships dedicated to retrieving various crashed rockets from the Baltic waves. The remote location, chosen by Wernher von Braun, facilitated secrecy, while the generally clear, excellent weather provided ample launch opportunities.

Exploring new technical frontiers as they did, the Germans naturally encountered many difficulties, producing "duds" which led to better designs. Von Braun remarked pithily about the first A-1 ("Aggragat 1") rocket that "it took us half a year to build and exactly one-half second to blow up." (Zaloga, 2003, 4). The final rocket received the designation A-4, though a half-size test-bed A-5 coexisted with it. The A-4 eventually received the famous designation V-2. A fresh face at the V-2 facility in 1943, Dieter Huzel, described his first view of these futuristic weapons: "I saw them—four, fantastic shapes but a few feet away, strange and towering above us in the subdued light. I could only think that they must be out of some science fiction film—Frau im Mond [The Woman in the Moon] brought to earth. I just stood and stared, my mouth hanging open for an exclamation that never emerged. [...] They were painted a dull olive green, and this, said Hartmut, as well as their shape, had won them the nickname of cucumber. I laughed, and the spell was broken."

The Peenemünde facility eventually employed over 3,000 scientists, engineers, and artisans, plus numerous slave laborers. The brilliant Silesian chemist and rocket scientist Walter Thiel took a leading role, developing a highly efficient liquid oxygen engine for the A-4/V-2 rocket, an improved combustion chamber, better fuel injectors, and short, wide engine nozzles that together produced powerful thrust with maximum fuel efficiency.

Thiel

Von Braun, in the meantime, headed research on guidance systems, while continuing to serve as the rocket program's "face" and liaison with the military and government due to his persuasive, easygoing manner. Other men contributed depending on their expertise. Moritz Pöhlmann developed "film cooling" for the combustion chamber, using an alcohol film to insulate the metal walls so that the intense flame of the rocket engine did not melt them. Teams of engineers produced graphite fins or vanes for the rockets and precisely calibrated turbines to manage exhaust flow.

In 1942, the Luftwaffe started a second rocketry program, creating the world's first cruise missile (just as the A-4/V-2 represented the first ballistic missile) – variously known as the Fieseler Fi-103, the V-1, and the "Buzz Bomb." Each rocket had strengths and weaknesses. V-1s proved very cheap and easy to manufacture, but they moved slowly enough for aircraft to potentially intercept them and shoot them down. V-2s demanded immense expenditure to produce, but they moved so quickly no defense then existing could shoot them down. The Third Reich's leaders opted to fund both programs, though Hitler shrank from issuing a mass production order for the V-2 before it proved any exceptional usefulness.

A V-1 rocket

The Peenemünde engineers even prepared a preliminary design for an intercontinental ballistic missile (ICBM) dubbed the "America Bomb" or A-10. However, the technology for such a device did not exist at the time. Von Braun's scientists lacked the years of design and experimentation needed to produce such a long-range rocket.

In 1940, Heinrich Himmler, wanting to extend SS influence to the rocket program, pressured Wernher von Braun into joining the organization despite his lack of political commitment. Von Braun joined chiefly to keep working on his passion, rocketry, but his eventual rise to the rank of Sturmbannführer (major) tainted his reputation and dogged him following the war.

A few years later, Arthur Rudolph and several other leading Peenemünde figures began using slave labor at the facility in 1942. Contrary to their later claims that Himmler forced this move on them, their letters and memos at the time indicate nothing but enthusiasm among this group's members for the use of Soviet, Polish, and French POWs for coerced labor. Von Braun seemingly had no hand in the decision, but little evidence exists that it particularly distressed him, either.

Regardless, the A-4/V-2 proved to be spectacular during launch, delighting the scientists who labored so long to produce it: "'It looked like a fiery sword going into the sky,' team member

Krafft Ehricke would recall years later. 'And then came this enormous roar. The whole sky seemed to vibrate. This kind of unearthly roaring was something human beings had never heard.'" (Spangenburg, 2008, 56).

The ballistic trajectory of a V-2 had an apogee of 58 miles and a maximum range of 200 miles. The rocket arrived at its target at 2,500 miles per hour, far too fast for aircraft or flak interception, and each missile strike came with essentially no warning that human synapses had time to respond to. Landing on open ground, a V-2 blew a crater 50 feet in diameter into the soil, while its mass and velocity permitted it to plunge all the way to a building's basement prior to detonation, demolishing even the sturdiest structures. Charles Ostyn, then an 18-year-old resident of Antwerp, later recalled what the arrival of a V-2 looked like: "I saw this flash during the day, but only once – I just happened to look at the sky in the right direction. It was definitely not a contrail, but it was like a streak from a comet – as fast as a shooting star. It was a long, thin, white streak, more like a flash coming down to the earth. This was seen about 1-2 seconds before the impact. When a V-2 rocket hit in the city it was always followed by a huge black or brownish cloud of debris."

The V-2's accuracy remained very poor, however, with misses of up to 14 miles and sometimes as much as 40 miles not uncommon. The Germans built, at the highest estimate, 6,915 V-2 rockets, a remarkable and remarkably wasteful feat given the 46-foot length and immense complexity of each missile. An estimated 3,225 rockets that reached their targets killed 2,700 British citizens. The effects in Antwerp, however, reached appalling levels - as many as 30,000 civilians and soldiers died in V-2 strikes, including 591 people killed on December 16, 1944 when a V-2 struck a packed theater, the "Rex Cinema," screening the Gary Cooper film *The Plainsman.* The rockets also sank at least 150 ships, and approximately 15,000 slave laborers died building the V-2s, a deadly effect which might perhaps also be counted among the weapon's death toll.

In the end, the V-2 provided an impressive display of technology's expanding potential, but it lacked the punch to achieve what Hitler wanted of it. Conventional warheads lacked the destructive power to make a limited number of ballistic missiles capable of forcing an enemy's surrender. Meanwhile, the German nuclear program remained so small that no chance existed of firing a ballistic atom bomb.

Of course, Churchill couldn't have known that with certainty, and he continued to fear the development of a nuclear weapon. The British had some intelligence regarding the *Uranprojekt* through their MI6 spy agency and the Special Operations Executive (SOE), but it was limited. Most frustratingly for Churchill, the bulk of the German nuclear weapons program was being conducted in the country's interior, making it virtually impossible to attack or impede.

The exception to this was the heavy water facility in Norway, and it was here that the British focused their actions. The Norsk Hydro Vemork plant was located on the very edge of the Third

Reich, and it was also just about within range of a British raid, the first of which was called Operation Freshman. Taking place in November 1942, the aim of the British was to damage the plant enough so as to derail or at least hold up the progress towards a bomb by restricting access to the key ingredient of heavy water.

The British became increasingly concerned about the *Uranprojekt* after receiving intelligence from a Norwegian resistance fighter, Leif Tronstad, who corresponded with London and revealed that heavy water production had intensified during 1941.[11] Tronstad had escaped the country across the border to Sweden and then to the UK, where he was a source of information and later the leader of the Norwegian sabotage teams, though he did not participate in the actions.[12]

Operation Freshman involved 34 commandos being flown to Norway in two military glider-aircraft combinations in an attempt to blow up the plant and escape across the border into Sweden. Although they made it to the Norwegian coast, bad weather and navigation problems caused the mission to go horribly wrong.[13] The gliders crashed, either killing the commandos outright or leading to their capture, after which they were tortured and executed.[14] It was a stark reminder of how dangerous any missions to sabotage the Nazi war effort were likely to prove.

Two subsequent attempts to damage the heavy water plant - Operation Grouse and Operation Gunnerside - proved more successful.[15] Britain's SOE had managed to recruit an engineer working at the facility, a Norwegian patriot named Einar Skinnarland, in March 1942. Skinnarland made it to Britain, trained there, and was sent back to Norway to infiltrate the German lines. Four other Norwegians also received British training before being transported back as part of Operation Grouse in October 1942. Intended to participate in the destruction of the heavy water plant, the Operation Grouse agents retreated into the wilderness following the failure of the two gliders in Operation Freshman.

Despite the Nazis now being aware that the heavy water facility was a target, the saboteurs evaded capture, lying in wait until the next attempt, Operation Gunnerside. British intelligence managed to ascertain that the Operation Grouse team had survived the reprisals meted out by the Nazis at the end of 1942 following the failed Operation Freshman. As a result, SOE dropped six

[11] "Operation Gunnerside", Atomic Heritage Foundation, https://www.atomicheritage.org/history/operation-gunnerside, [accessed 7 June 2019]

[12] "Operation Gunnerside", Atomic Heritage Foundation, https://www.atomicheritage.org/history/operation-gunnerside, [accessed 7 June 2019]

[13] Damien Lewis, "The Third Reich's nuclear program: Churchill's greatest wartime fear", *History Extra*, 22 March 2018, https://www.historyextra.com/period/second-world-war/the-third-reichs-nuclear-program-churchills-greatest-wartime-fear/, [accessed 3 June 2019]

[14] Damien Lewis, "The Third Reich's nuclear program: Churchill's greatest wartime fear", *History Extra*, 22 March 2018, https://www.historyextra.com/period/second-world-war/the-third-reichs-nuclear-program-churchills-greatest-wartime-fear/, [accessed 3 June 2019]

[15] Damien Lewis, "The Third Reich's nuclear program: Churchill's greatest wartime fear", *History Extra*, 22 March 2018, https://www.historyextra.com/period/second-world-war/the-third-reichs-nuclear-program-churchills-greatest-wartime-fear/, [accessed 3 June 2019]

more Norwegian resistance fighters into Norway on February 16, 1943 as part of Operation Gunnerside. The two groups linked up and prepared to attack the heavy water facility on February 27, despite the fact it had been reinforced with landmines and extra guards after the previous British-backed effort.

Nine Norwegians embarked upon Operation Gunnerside on February 27 in one of the most celebrated undercover operations of the war. The nine agents' mission was to sabotage the Norsk Hydro plant, just outside the town of Rjukan. Leif Tronstad, who still guided the mission from Britain, advised against any plan to bomb the facility, believing it would lead to loss of civilian life and ultimately be ineffective.[16]

Led on the ground by Joachim Rønneberg, part of the second group who landed in mid-February, the team opted to avoid the minefield by climbing down a nearby gorge and then scaling a cliff about 500 feet high. The team used wire cutters to break through the facility's perimeter fence and divided into two groups, a covering group essentially on lookout and a smaller group responsible for getting into the main building and laying explosive charges close to the heavy water production cells.[17]

The charges were detonated and damaged the production of the heavy water while the entire Norwegian team slipped away into the wilderness on skis and across the border into Sweden. It was an astonishing success, which frustrated but also impressed the Nazis when they discovered the damage to the plant.[18] Operation Gunnerside was a serious blow to the Nazis production of heavy water and a setback for the *Uranprojekt*, but it only set the plant back months without actually destroying its capacity.[19] The Nazis attempted to shift heavy water production from Norway to Germany, including transporting a ferry of semi-refined product in early 1944. That too was sabotaged by the Norwegians, who planted a bomb on the boat and managed to sink the ferry.[20]

Historians have debated the extent to which these secret sabotage missions altered the course of the war. Some believe that they were decisive in holding up the development of a German nuclear weapon and potentially were all-important in the war's final outcome. Others claim that by 1943 the Nazis were already winding down the *Uranprojekt* and therefore these missions had little overall effect. In any case, there is little doubt concerning the bravery and the derring-do of

---

[16] "Operation Gunnerside", Atomic Heritage Foundation, https://www.atomicheritage.org/history/operation-gunnerside, [accessed 7 June 2019]

[17] "Operation Gunnerside", Atomic Heritage Foundation, https://www.atomicheritage.org/history/operation-gunnerside, [accessed 7 June 2019]

[18] Neal Bascomb, *The Winter Fortress: The Epic Mission to Sabotage Hitler's Atomic Bomb* (Mariner Books, 2017), p. 213.

[19] "Operation Gunnerside", Atomic Heritage Foundation, https://www.atomicheritage.org/history/operation-gunnerside, [accessed 7 June 2019]

[20] "Operation Gunnerside", Atomic Heritage Foundation, https://www.atomicheritage.org/history/operation-gunnerside, [accessed 7 June 2019]

the commandos involved, and the operation unsurprisingly became the subject of films and books, including *The Heroes of Telemark* (1965), *A Man Called Intrepid* (1979) and the more recent miniseries *The Heavy Water War* (2015). Joachim Rønneberg himself was the last of the commandos to pass away, dying in October 2018 at the age of 99.

Recent research on the Nazi *Uranprojekt* has led to some startling assertions. Most notable among these are the claims by German historian Rainer Karlsch that the Nazis actually conducted a number of nuclear tests in 1944 and 1945. In his book *Hitler's Bomb*, Karlsch asserts that his research suggested that the Nazis, despite having a fraction of the Manhattan Project's manpower and budget, managed to accelerate their nuclear program to the testing stage out of desperation.[21] It should be stated here that Karlsch's claims have been met with widespread criticism, and he has acknowledged the unsubstantiated nature of the narrative.[22]

Certainly, Hitler was becoming increasingly desperate in 1944, particularly after the D-Day landings in Northern France. As the Allies closed in, it seemed only a matter of time before Nazi Germany would face its final reckoning. Hitler and his fanatical associates, however, far from preparing for this eventuality or even seeking peace negotiations, became more extreme in the final months of the war. Teenagers and in some cases even children were sent to fight and "defend" the Reich as part of a "People's Army," in many instances being sent to their certain deaths while the Holocaust was ramped up. It would therefore be entirely in character if the Nazis had made a final desperate attempt to develop a nuclear bomb, or even a "dirty bomb."[23]

Karlsch's main claim is that the Nazis detonated several nuclear explosions at the end of 1944 and beginning of 1945 in the state of Thüringen, in central-eastern Germany.[24] He also outlined how concentration camp prisoners were forced to work on the nuclear project at Thüringen, overseen by the SS, and even incinerated during the explosions.[25] Other documents potentially supporting the tests include a GRU (Soviet intelligence) report from late 1944 claiming that the Nazis were about to conduct a nuclear test, based upon a fission reaction.[26] Hitler is also alleged to have told the Romanian leader Ion Antonescu about new V-3 and V-4 rockets, insinuating that they were armed with nuclear bombs. The latter point is perhaps somewhat moot as Hitler was presumably trying to keep Antonescu on his side at a time when the Romanians were seeking an

---

[21] Klaus Wiegrefe, How Close Was Hitler to the A-Bomb?, *Der Spiegel*, 14 March 2005, https://www.spiegel.de/international/spiegel/the-third-reich-how-close-was-hitler-to-the-a-bomb-a-346293.html, [accessed 3 June 2019]

[22] Jeremy Bernstein, *Plutonium: A History of the World's Most Dangerous Element*, (University of NSW Press, 2009), p. x.

[23] Andreas Sulzer, Stefan Brauburger, Christian Frey, *Secrets of the Third Reich: The Search for Hitler's Bomb* (Documentary Film)

[24] Jeremy Bernstein, *Plutonium: A History of the World's Most Dangerous Element*, (University of NSW Press, 2009), p. x.

[25] Andreas Sulzer, Stefan Brauburger, Christian Frey, *Secrets of the Third Reich: The Search for Hitler's Bomb* (Documentary Film)

[26] Andreas Sulzer, Stefan Brauburger, Christian Frey, *Secrets of the Third Reich: The Search for Hitler's Bomb* (Documentary Film)

exit strategy from the war. Needless to say, Hitler was not known for his honesty.

Karlsch's claims about the Thüringen nuclear tests have not been proven. If they did take place, the entire nuclear weapons program was wound down in the first months of 1945, Germany was invaded, facilities were occupied, and the military was disrupted. By this point, the Nazi leadership was engaged in a suicide mission, with Hitler confined to his Berlin bunker giving increasingly unrealistic orders. A state of anarchy descended over Germany in the final months of the war, and in its aftermath, Nazi scientists were also facing a reckoning of their own.

British Transfer Policies

In the wake of World War I, John Maynard Keynes warned against French demands at Versailles for punitive cash reparations and the seizure of Germany's raw materials. He foresaw the resulting financial collapse, but his views had little impact and the French got their way claiming reparations estimated at $30 billion dollars. Keynes responded by publishing "The Economic Consequences of the Peace." As Keynes predicted, the Germans were unable to keep up payments, and France and Belgium reoccupied the Ruhr in 1923 to force their hand leading to strikes and hyperinflation.

It is an oversimplification to say that this led directly to the rise of Hitler and World War II, but it contributed to the problems and proved Keynes right. As such, his view that cash reparations were counterproductive had become received wisdom on both sides of the Atlantic by the time planning for the aftermath of World War II began in earnest in 1943. Allied leaders thus looked at other ways to punish Germany and recover some of the costs of war.[27]

The reallocation of territory as reparations was another issue that had not worked out well after Versailles. The collapse of the Austro-Hungarian and Ottoman empires led to the creation of a plethora of new states, but many of these proved unstable and their disputed boundaries led to further conflict. After 1945, the creation of new states was avoided in Western Europe, where the British focus was always to reconstitute and rebuild existing states. However, in 1945, as in 1919, huge swathes of territory were reallocated elsewhere as a form of reparations. The Russians deprived Germany of almost a third of its prewar land area east of the Oder-Neisse line and regarded these ceded territories as a form of reparations to be controlled politically and exploited economically.[28]

One consequence of Russian territorial acquisition was that displaced populations became more pressing issues after 1945, and the refugee crisis would force the Allies into improvised measures on a massive scale.

---

[27] Morgenthau, Henry. 1944. "Suggested Post Surrender Program for Germany". *Waybackmachine*. https://web.archive.org/web/20130531235410/http://docs.fdrlibrary.marist.edu/psf/box31/t297a01.htm.
[28] Naimark.

Each group of displaced persons (DP) had a significant effect on British reparations and reconstruction policy.[29] The first group consisted intellectuals who had fled Nazi Germany and Austria in the 1930s. Many of these were taken into government service in World War II and played an important role in both direct technology transfer and the management of the British zone of occupation, as well as the harnessing of German science and technology as contacts, sources of cultural knowledge and translators.

However, the role of these prewar refugees was overshadowed by millions of new DPs from two additional sources. The first were the slave laborers from all over occupied Europe abandoned by the retreating Nazis. Many of these had worked in facilities targeted by the Allies as military booty or civilian reparations and remained clustered in the localities while British reparation forces were at work.[30] The second group were people, often entire families, fleeing ahead of the advance of the Soviet armies across Eastern Europe in 1944-1945 and the Soviets' subsequent annexation of territories. Both groups of DPs became the responsibility of the three Western occupying powers, but nobody had considered who should bear the cost of feeding and housing them, or how meeting their needs would affect the selfish desires of the Allies to denude Germany of resources in the form of reparations.

A third area in which 1940s planners felt mistakes had been made at Versailles was the absence of the military occupation of Germany. The British did occupy the Ruhr in 1918-1919 but soon withdrew, and the French and Belgians then reoccupied the area in 1923 in a catastrophic attempt to speed up reparation payments. However, the rest of the country escaped military occupation, and by the 1940s this was widely believed to have facilitated the *Dolchstosslegende* ("stab in the back") myth exploited by Hitler in his rise to power. According to Wheeler Bennett (1954), this was seen as a mistake the Allies would not repeat by insisting that "it was necessary for the Nazi régime and/or the German Generals to surrender unconditionally in order to bring home to the German people that they had lost the war by themselves; so that their defeat should not be attributed to a 'stab in the back.'"[31]

Consequently, one of the first joint decisions taken regarding the postwar future of Germany was to divide it into zones of occupation. At the Tehran Conference in November 1943, three zones were planned, and a fourth French zone was added at Yalta in February 1945. This zonal approach to managing postwar Germany ultimately defined the area from which each power could obtain personnel, IP, and equipment, but the spatial location was not quite that simple because in the chaos of the final weeks of the Third Reich, the troops did not always halt on the agreed boundary lines. Withdrawals to the agreed lines were subsequently negotiated by the end of July 1945, but in those months, having troops on the ground created a vital opportunity to

[29] The term *displaced persons* is used in almost all official British documents of the time and has been adopted here in preference to refugees for the sake of authenticity and inclusiveness.
[30] Longden.
[31] Wheeler Bennett, John. 1954. *The Nemesis of Power, The German Army in Politics, 1918-1945.* 1st ed. London: Macmillan.

extend the scope of seizures of personnel, IP and equipment, just as the British did before the evacuation of the Magdeburg Bulge and Schwerin Pocket.[32]

Furthermore, since all the Allies retained rights to visit sights of scientific interest in each other's zones subject to diplomatic protocols, there were tensions among them, and none of the powers, including the British, fully entered into the spirit of this agreement. Obstruction of access and unauthorized raids to seize personnel, particularly by the Russians, became a feature of the occupation and a way in which transfer policies contributed to the descent into the Cold War.[33]

Planning for the aftermath of World War II was strongly influenced by a fourth perceived mistake made at Versailles: the naive assumption that what had just happened was the "war to end all wars" and must never be allowed to happen again. Most hardware surrendered in 1918 was scrapped as quickly as possible, and the public mood was for disarmament, not the exploitation of captured technology to develop new and more deadly weapons. In any case the Entente Powers were confident that they had the technological advantage in most of the key areas such as tanks, aircraft and wireless.

After 1945, the mood was different. The political and military leaders of Britain and the USA expected another war against the Soviet Union imminently, and their people were willing to go along with this.[34] For their part, the Russian leaders aggressively planned to catch up with the USA and Britain technically in order to retain and expand the zone of influence they had acquired in Eastern Europe. Thus, all the victorious powers were motivated to expropriate equipment and IP and persuade or force German experts to assist the development of their future military capability and economic recovery.

The Versailles settlement also left a sense of injustice among the British, who felt that nobody had been held accountable for causing the First World War. The Allies intended for the end of World War II to be different by preparing for war crimes prosecutions and programs to change the mindset of individuals through denazification. The impetus for justice in this sense increased as the scale of the Holocaust and other atrocities gradually became known to the general public in late 1944 and 1945.[35] At the same time, the aims of justice and economic advantage would come into conflict.

Of course, British and other allied efforts to access German technology and scientists was the general belief that the Germans were superior in many respects. The crews of Matilda and

---

[32] Longden.

[33] Naimark.

[34] Hennessy, Peter. 1992. *Never Again*. London: J. Cape.

[35] A clear summary of the vast literature on this topic is Redmond, Caroline. 2019. "The Nuremberg Trials: When the World Tried to Bring the Nazis to Justice and Failed". Blog. *All That's Interesting*. https://allthatsinteresting.com/nuremberg-trials.

Churchill tanks were outrun and outgunned by German Panzer IV and Panther tanks. Royal Air Force pilots were unable to keep up with the first operational jet fighter, the Messerschmitt ME 262, and the British were painfully aware that Germany had been the first to develop a ballistic missile.

There was also a strong belief among some British industrial circles in German superiority.[36] One source was prewar visits such as those made by Roy Fedden, chief designer of the Bristol radial aircraft engines to the BMW aero engine factory in 1937, which left him deeply impressed. It is not a coincidence that he led the "Fedden Mission," sponsored by the Ministry of Supply (MoS), to investigate German aircraft and aero engine production and technology in August 1945.[37] Another source of business and civil service belief in German technical superiority was the Germans' ability to maintain production despite relentless bombing and the blockade that attempted to deprive them of essential raw materials.

Fedden

In official circles British transfers between 1944 and 1949 were never seen purely as plunder. The success of the code breakers at Bletchley Park convinced officialdom that World War II was an intelligence war more than anything that had gone before and future wars would be even more intelligence led. Therefore, a primary motive in the British transfer policy was always intelligence gathering and the reason units developed to carry out the transfers originated in the intelligence establishment.[38]

---

[36] Longden.
[37] Coneybeare, John. 2011. "Sir Roy Fedden (1885-1973)". Blog. *Engineer's Walk.*
   http://www.engineerswalk.co.uk/rf_walk.html.
[38] Hall, Chapter 2.

Denying access to the other Allies in British spheres of influence was an increasingly important motive throughout the period of British transfers from Germany, but it was not always the Russians who were to be denied. For the first eight months of 1945, until the use of the atomic bombs averted the need for amphibious assaults on the Dutch East Indies and the Japanese mainland, the principal objective was to identify what naval technology (such as new types of torpedoes, gunsights and mines) the Germans had shared with the Japanese and deny the Japanese more of it.[39] Before the Russians entered center stage, the planners feared that "Britain would be incredibly vulnerable to attack by a weapon about which they knew nothing,"[40] meaning some kind of "wonder weapon" in the hands of Nazi fanatics popularly known as *werewolves*. Today this sounds like fantasy, but the military orders of the time make it clear that the threat was taken very seriously.

If there was one single event which marked the shift of denial strategies from the Japanese and the werewolves to the Russians, it was the raid on Kiel, which occurred on May 4, 1945. This crucial port was officially in the British zone, but as part of the ceasefire, British troops were ordered to stop 40 miles short, leaving open the possibility of a Russian advance. This was contrary to the Yalta agreement, but it provided the Russians a potential opportunity to sieze the entire Baltic coast, the Kiel Canal, and Denmark, along with vital sites and technology along the way, including the *Walther-Werke* advanced engine factory and U- boat construction yards in Kiel. Most of the British high command were still willing to trust the Russians not to do so, but somebody, still unidentified, ordered T-Force under Major Hibbert to ignore the ceasefire and seize Kiel to deny it to the Russians. They did so, and the Russians chose not to risk a confrontation.

If the Russians really had intended to capture the Baltic coast and Denmark, which has never been proved, then this denial operation changed the entire history of Northern Europe fundamentally. Major Hibbert was arrested by the Military Police but never court-martialed. From then on, awareness grew rapidly that denying Nazi technology to the Russians was now one of the major motives for the British transfer policy.

The British were clear about the motives of their transfer program, and, after Yalta, they had a clearly defined zone to occupy but did not have a clear plan about how to manage that zone. In fact, Britain never issued a single, all-encompassing plan for the postwar management of Germany, and there was never an Act of Parliament setting out the principles. Throughout this time, the Americans took the initiative in strategic planning and Britain largely followed American principles.

The genesis of American thinking was the Morgenthau Plan, originally entitled "Suggested Post-Surrender Plan for Germany." This was the work of Henry Morgenthau, Jr., a New Deal

---

[39] Longden.
[40] Hall, 18.

economist and Secretary of the Treasury, and it focused on four aspects of the management of postwar Germany which would be central to the Allies. These aspects included the repudiation of cash reparations, ideological cleansing, the deindustrialization of Germany, and international cooperation.[41] Of these, denazification and deindustrialization were the most contentious, and the conflict between ideals and reality in both areas had a major influence on the implementation of the British transfer policies.

Unlike Morgenthau, Roosevelt believed that the German people collectively shared in the guilt of the Nazi regime and needed to be made to face up to the affront to civilization that they had taken part in.[42] The British concurred, and the term adopted for this program of ideological cleansing, denazification, originated in the Pentagon in 1943 as part of a plan to purge the German legal profession. In the ensuing years, it was swiftly widened into a joint initiative to eradicate from German society, culture, press, economy, judiciary, and politics all remnants of Nazi ideology by removing from positions of authority anyone who had had been a Nazi Party member and by disbanding and outlawing the organizations through which Nazism permeated German society. [43]

---

[41] Morgenthau, Henry. 1944. "Suggested Post Surrender Program for Germany". *Waybackmachine*. https://web.archive.org/web/20130531235410/http://docs.fdrlibrary.marist.edu/psf/box31/t297a01.htm. It is important to consult the original text here cited because the Morgenthau Plan is often confused with JCS1067, A Handbook for Military government in Germany." In fact, there were fundamental differences and Morgenthau repudiated JCS1067.

[42] Alliierten Museum. 2019. "Denazification | Alliiertenmuseum Berlin". *Alliiertenmuseum.De*. http://www.alliiertenmuseum.de/en/topics/denazification.html.

[43] Taylor, Frederick. 2011. *Exorcising Hitler: The Occupation and Denazification of Germany*. Bloomsbury Publishing.

Morgenthau, Jr.

However, the Yalta Agreement laid down few details regarding precisely how this would be done, leaving ample scope for divergent British and American interpretations.[44] The notebooks of the Cabinet Secretary show that when the mechanics of denazification were discussed in April 1945, Churchill initially favored summary execution of major criminals using an electric chair borrowed from the United States.[45] Conversely, Roosevelt and then Truman, a former judge, persuaded both Churchill and Stalin that due process of the law had to be followed. The British then took the lead in joint preparations for war crimes prosecutions, leading to the promulgation of the London Charter of the International Military Tribunal in early August 1945. That set out the procedure for the Nuremberg Trials.

The Versailles Treaty had restricted the number and type of weapons Germany could legally possess, as well as the size of its army, but it had not deprived Germany of the industrial capacity to make weapons if it chose to ignore the treaty stipulations, as the Nazis did. Consequently,

---

[44] For the full text of the Yalta agreement see: Avalon Project. 2008. "The Avalon Project: Yalta (Crimea) Conference". *Avalon.Law.Yale.Edu*. https://avalon.law.yale.edu/wwii/yalta.asp.

[45] Cabinet Office. 2019. "WWII British War Cabinet Notebooks". *Paperlessarchives.Com*. Accessed June 24. http://paperlessarchives.com/wwii_british_war_cabinet_.html.

Morgenthau envisaged "the total destruction of the whole German armament industry, and the removal or destruction of other key industries which are basic to military strength."[46] These efforts would be concentrated in the Ruhr, which Morgenthau stated should be completely stripped within six months of occupation.[47] The British initially agreed with this view, which in practice meant reducing postwar Germany to an agrarian society.

Morgenthau considered several other aspects of the postwar economy and potential reparations. He rejected transfers of cash or raw materials following Keynesian thinking,[48] as well as any form of forced labor by Germans outside Germany as a form of reparations. However, Morgenthau did envisage reparations in the form of the return of assets looted by the Germans from occupied territory and the confiscation of all German assets held abroad.[49]

After much debate within the Roosevelt administration and the resignation of Morgenthau, a modified form of his plan emerged as an order known as Joint Chiefs of Staff (JCS) 1067, secretly issued to Eisenhower sometime in the spring of 1945 and officially titled "A Handbook for Military Government in Germany." This did not significantly change the nature of reparations envisaged but did go even further in denying Germany an economic future by stating that the military government must not take any steps aimed at the economic rehabilitation of Germany or the maintenance and strengthening of the German economy.[50]

JCS1067 was never issued to British troops and technically only applied to the American zone, but Eisenhower was instructed that "you will urge the adoption by the other occupying powers of the principles and policies set forth in this directive."[51] President Truman, who replaced Roosevelt after his death in office in April 1945, succeeded in getting British Prime Minister Clement Attlee, who replaced Churchill on July 26, 1945, to agree to the main principles at Potsdam that August.

The wartime British coalition government did develop a substantial economic planning apparatus for managing UK production and distribution, but, surprisingly, it never produced a coherent plan for the economic future of postwar Germany. Thus, JCS1067 became, ostensibly, the main instrument of British as well as American occupation policy even as the two sides did not practice the policy in the same manner on the ground. By the time it was put into practice in the American zone in the summer of 1945, the British had demonstrated their lack of faith in planning and had begun several aspects of the transfer policy using ad hoc organizations and an inductive, evidence-led approach which often sat uneasily with the plans imposed. The problem

---

[46] Morgenthau, Clause 1
[47] Ibid, Clause 3
[48] Ibid. Clause 4
[49] Ibid. Clause 4e
[50] JCS1067. 2008. "Avalon Project - Directive to Commander-In-Chief of United States Forces of Occupation Regarding the Military Government Of Germany; April 1945". *Avalon.Law.Yale.Edu.* https://avalon.law.yale.edu/wwii/ger02.asp.
[51] https://en.wikisource.org/wiki/JCS_1067 contains the full text.

was that the ideals of reducing Germany to a harmless, agrarian society took no account of the huge influx of displaced populations from the east, which overwhelmed the capacity of a purely agrarian economy to feed them.

Many of the management policies for postwar Germany were forced to adapt to this reality. For example, as early as October 17, 1945 Lord Templewood moved a motion in the House of Lords stating, "It is essential that, subject to the overriding claim of security, the fullest possible use should be made of the industrial resources of Germany for the purpose of economic recovery, and that His Majesty's Government, being primarily responsible for a zone in which a great part of these resources is concentrated, should regularly publish reports as to the course of employment and production in the zone, the state of the population and the extent of the contribution made by the zone towards the economic needs of the Continent."[52]

In the debate that followed, he argued that German raw materials, especially coal, were irreplaceable, and that it was essential to get German industry up and running again to restore European trade. He further argued, quoting reports from Eisenhower, that Britain would have to pay for the large-scale imports of food to Germany to feed everyone, which it could ill afford to do. These considerations, Lord Templewood argued, should be taken into account in British reparations and denazification policies. Not all his fellow peers agreed, but in practice his views did become the background to the remainder of the British transfer policy in occupied Germany, especially as the Treasury persistently sought to reduce the costs of the British occupation.[53]

The British took part in the creation of two key interallied organizations long before the actual defeat of Germany. These were not planning bodies but intelligence gathering bodies. The first was the Combined Intelligence Directives Sub-Committee (CIOS), which was set up in July 1944 and was comprised of teams of military and civilian technical experts who reported to the Supreme Headquarters Allied Expeditionary Force (SHAEF), the military command for the invasion and conquest of occupied Europe and Germany itself. Many of the personnel involved were prewar refugees from Germany and Austria engaged for their German language skills and knowledge of German industrial and scientific infrastructure. Its main contribution was to draw up lists of technologies, companies, and individuals the Allies wished to seize and learn from. This was done using open source intelligence, such as academic publications by German scientists, as well as aerial reconnaissance photographs and reports from European resistance groups. The results were prioritized and put into black folders, which became known as the "black list" of targets. There was also a much larger "grey list" of lower priority, mostly industrial targets, and both lists were continually updated as more intelligence became available.[54]

The second organization set up in advance of the defeat of Germany was Target Force (T-

---

[52] HL Deb 17 October 1945 vol 137 cc321-53.
[53] Hennessey.
[54] Hall, Chapters 2-3.

Force), and thanks to the research of Longden (2009) and Hall (2019), a great deal is now known about how T-Force was organized and operated. T-Force was a military unit set up to gather intelligence in the field from targets that had previously been identified by CIOS. It was a large and organized body embedded with the front-line troops and formed from a unique mixture of the remnants of broken infantry battalions, soldiers recovering from battlefield injuries both physical and psychological, bomb disposal experts to deal with booby traps, intelligence and technical experts, translators, and career criminals freed from jail to carry out specialist functions such as blowing safes. In the field, T-Force operated in small teams known as Consolidated Advance Field Teams (CAFT), and their job was to seize and secure factories, weapons sites, and archives, prevent them from being destroyed by retreating Germans, looted by Allied troops or refugees, and deny them to the werewolves or Russians. T-Force units had their own transport and were highly mobile.

Although they were supplied with target lists by CIOS, it was recognized that the intelligence was incomplete. Surviving records and memoirs make it clear that T-Force operations were often ad hoc and policy was made on the hoof. Junior officers were given a great deal of initiative to investigate additional "opportunity targets" and subject to minimal central planning or coordination.[55] This was sound policy, and these opportunity targets turned out to include some of the biggest finds of the war, such as the Luftwaffe Research Centre at Völkenrode, a facility whose existence had been successfully camouflaged.[56]

Once operations commenced after D-Day, T-Force also developed a sizable back office function. Once a target had been secured, T-Force would call in civilian "assessors," scientists and technical experts seconded from the civil service, the armed forces, or civilian industry on an ad hoc basis. T-Force was responsible for organizing the logistics of their visits, including transport, food, accommodation, armed escorts, and so on. When on site investigations were complete, T-Force troops packed documents, prototypes, and machinery for shipment back to Britain via its own network of warehouses. T-Force units also ran detention centers for German personnel detained for interrogation in Germany and arranged the rendition of those taken to England for questioning.

Meanwhile, the British also made plans to implement another of Morgenthau's proposed reparations: the confiscation of prewar German assets held in the UK. The official view on this matter evolved in the form of various Regulations promulgated under the Trading with the Enemy Act, 1939. By 1944, the position envisaged by the Treasury was more complex and nuanced than the Morgenthau Plan. Essentially, assets belonging to "belligerent enemies" would be confiscated and used to offset British war costs at least until a permanent peace treaty could be signed.

---

[55] Christopher, John. 2013. *The Race for Hitler's X-Planes.* London: Trafalgar Square Publishing; Howard; Longden.
[56] Christopher.

Provisions were made to release assets to assist refugees, but it was decided in July 1943 and September 1944 (Regulations 6 and 7) that assets belonging to residents of formerly German-occupied countries remained under the custodianship of British banks until the Board of Trade decreed otherwise. The authorities were aware of the possible political fallout but feared aiding collaborators and Nazis seeking to launder money for their escape.[57] The effect was inevitably to slow reconstruction, but it did marginally offset Britain's chronic financial difficulties.

British Areas of Interest

As ad hoc British transfer policies went ahead shortly after D-Day in liberated France and gathered pace as British forces entered Germany itself in the winter of 1944-1945, CIOS identified key areas of British interest classified "A1" in the black List. These included the following:

- Aerodynamics
- Chemical weapons
- Infra-red and night fighting equipment
- Jet engines
- Nuclear weapons
- Radar
- Rocket technology
- Submarine warfare
- Synthetic materials especially rubber

Within each category target sites were identified which T-Force sought to occupy as quickly as possible. In some cases, key personnel had also been identified in advance and early detainees supplied networks of further contacts under interrogation.[58]

As the war neared its end, the areas of interest shifted away from purely military research to infrastructure, and T-Force was tasked with capturing and protecting from looting or sabotage all installations essential to the functioning of the postwar military government, especially post offices, telephone exchanges, and radio stations. This made a substantial contribution to the return of normality, but only by compromising non-fraternization and denazification rules. German staff often had to be left in posts to show Allied technicians how to operate the facilities, and some local German police were even allowed to keep their weapons and act as guards because T-Force lacked sufficient manpower.[59]

The return of peace brought a further shift in British areas of interest towards technologies of benefit to civilian industry. Major areas of interest included:
- Petrochemicals

---

[57] Foreign and Commonwealth Office. 1998. "British Policy Towards Enemy Property During and After the Second World War". History Notes. London.
[58] Longden.
[59] Ibid.

- Electronics
- Metallurgy
- Production processes
- Optics
- Synthetic materials.[60]

Transfer Organizations

One of the difficulties of getting an overview of the nature, extent, and impact of British transfers is the high number of organizations involved at different times, some with conflicting agendas, and the many acronyms they used.

As noted before, the early stages of planning in 1944-45 were the responsibility of the CIOS, a multinational body responsible to SHAEF, which controlled the field operational units of T-Force.[61] However, once the national zones of occupation were formally established in May 1945, SHAEF and CIOS were abolished. Within the British zone, CIOS was replaced by the British Intelligence Objectives Sub-Committee (BIOS), which was responsible to the Cabinet. It included representatives of each of the three services and MI6, which ran Operation Dustbin (intended to counter Russian attempts to persuade or force German experts wanted by Britain to work for the Russians instead).

Some key government departments were represented on BIOS. Given the always critical food, raw materials, and logistics situation, the Ministry of Supply (MoS) was the most important. Subordinate to the MoS representative on BIOS, the Scientific and Technical Research Board (STRB) sought the transfer of German experts, IP, and equipment to civilian industries whereas T-Force had previously been more focused on military technologies. Also represented on BIOS was the Board of Trade (BoT), which had a vested interest in restarting German industry and increasing prosperity in order to create an export market for British goods, contrary to the stated intention in JCS1067 of converting postwar Germany into an agrarian society.

Significantly, the Foreign and Commonwealth Office (FCO), which was responsible for dealing with the emerging Cold War, was not represented on BIOS. Neither was the Treasury, which was consistently trying to reduce the cost of the military occupation in ways which conflicted with both denazification and the desire to reduce Germany to an agrarian society.[62] In the matter of denazification, the wishes of the Treasury, the MoS and T-Force sometimes also came into conflict with the occupying forces, officially renamed the British Army of the Rhine (BAOR) after August 25, 1945. The BAOR remained in charge of denazification and war crimes

---

[60] Ibid.

[61] The names given to these organizations changed several times in their formative stages. In this paper I have used the names which have become standardized in the literature. For more details on the evolutionary process see Hall, 40-44.

[62] Hennessy.

prosecutions of all lower level Nazi personnel, which interfered with efforts to transfer people to the UK and to use them to restart German industry and infrastructure.

After SHAEF and CIOS were abolished, they were replaced by the Allied Control Council (ACC), the Field Intelligence Agency (Technical) (FIAT), and the Inter Allied Reparations Agency (IARA). The ACC was set up in May 1945 and was intended to be a body to negotiate and coordinate general policy between the four victorious powers, but as the Cold War mentality took hold, it became a forum to air their disputes.

FIAT was set up at the same time and had both British and American branches. FIAT and BIOS had offices in the same building in Baker Street, London and were capable of cooperation, for example in identifying experts of interest and even sending joint teams of investigators to some sites. That said, Longden (2009) and Christopher (2013) both cited numerous instances of rivalry and stonewalling.

The specific issue of reparations was coordinated by IARA, set up in the spring of 1946 with headquarters in Brussels to enforce a distinction between "booty" (military hardware) and "reparations" (goods transferred for civilian use to offset the cost of war damage), and to apportion reparations between the 18 countries with claims against Nazi Germany. Intangible assets, such as personnel and IP, were excluded from each country's reparation allowance, which tended to increase their attractiveness.[63]

Moreover, there were separate agencies collecting information about bomb damage and many others. Hall (2019) identified no less than 52 separate agencies operating in occupied Germany from 1945-1947, many of which were more intent on preserving their own bureaucratic fiefdoms than cooperating for the collective good.[64] This structure grew up ad hoc, and there were hundreds of parliamentary questions asked about detailed issues arising from transfers, but Parliament never debated the principles or a coherent plan to execute them. In practice, it was often unclear, even to officers on the ground, how all the different organizations were supposed to interact.[65] This meant there was duplication, confusion, and waste while important personnel, documents, and equipment slipped through Britain's fingers.[66] This was symptomatic of the point hammered home by Hennessey (1992) that the Attlee government had a very underdeveloped conception of planning (despite their socialist credentials) and lacked the means to develop or execute a broad, coherent plan.

None of the accounts published so far offers a schematic model of British transfers, but four main deficiencies are often implicit. Firstly, the meaning of looting is not always clear. What was

---

[63] IARA. 2019. "Inter-Allied Reparation Agency: Papers of UK Delegation | The National Archives". *Discovery.Nationalarchives.Gov.Uk*. https://discovery.nationalarchives.gov.uk/details/r/C14031.
[64] Hall, 76-78.
[65] Howard.
[66] Christopher.

regarded as capture of essential military technology by T-Force was often regarded as looting by other units but was carried out according to orders.[67] That is different from unauthorized looting by individual troops, which also happened on a substantial scale.[68] In the same vein, the distinction between booty and reparations imposed by IARA is also often overlooked, as are reparations in the form of confiscation of prewar financial assets and other financial issues.

British Methods

During the war, soldiers at the front often bypassed factories and offices, and T-Force troops following close behind would take possession of these. Frequently, armed German units were present, but T-Force rarely had to fight their way into a target. In most cases the German occupiers were eager to surrender, and bomb disposal experts would then check the building for booby traps. T-Force then overturned thousands of years of military tradition by preserving enemy lives and property instead of killing and destroying. Other units found this hard to accept, especially given the Nazis' policies of torture and summary execution, so T-Force had to be given authority from a very high level to keep other troops and displaced people out to prevent looting.[69]

At the same time, the treatment of DPs gave rise to one of the ethical criticisms of the British transfer policy, which consistently prioritized the needs of British military intelligence over the needs of the refugees. They were usually former slave laborers, often homeless and close to starvation, but they were still typically ejected with no attempt made to provide for their humanitarian needs.[70]

Once secured, the target was then searched by subject specific assessors. Locks and safes were blown open, if necessary, but other destruction was avoided and documents were kept together for dispatch to a processing center at Fort Halstead, Kent. In doing this, the British transfer policy showed no regard whatsoever for intellectual property rights (IPR). This was a much less developed legal concept in the 1940s than it is now, and, in any case, one of the first actions of the British military government, in Control Order Number 2, was to legalize all British transfers of tangible and intangible assets.[71] Small items of machinery and prototypes were similarly packed and sent to Britain intact. Larger items were dismantled but in ways that enabled them to be reassembled in the UK.[72]

The Germans rarely considered British seizures worth resisting or challenging legally. They just got on with replacing what was taken and in so doing leapfrogged the British technologically.[73] This process was made easier by the fact that, once emptied, civilian buildings

---

[67] Ibid.
[68] Hall, 212.
[69] Longden.
[70] Ibid.
[71] Allied Control Council.
[72] Longden.

were usually returned to German ownership rather than being leveled, a decision which contributed substantially to German reconstruction.

Most of the controversy surrounds the transfers of individuals. When a site was secured, key scientists, engineers, and managers were detained and interrogated. For most this took place in Germany, but those considered of the highest value were sent to Britain. In this context, the terms detained, interrogated, sent to Britain, and recruited have been used by historians without considering the full context.

There is very little information in memoirs or official documents about what precisely detention meant. In the early stages of T-Force operations, it is not entirely clear where prisoners were detained. Local military headquarters are the most likely. After Germany surrendered, T-Force acquired permanent prisons. Some were in Germany, such as the prison at Schloss Kransberg known as the Dustbin, where MI6 also carried out their detention and interrogation denial operations. Detention centers in the UK, particularly Spedan Towers in Hampstead, were also used extensively for interrogations.

The legality of British detentions in Britain or Germany was always dubious. T-Force soldiers and civilians were not police officers and had no legal powers of arrest. Most of those they wished to question were civilians, so the normal procedures of surrender and POW status did not apply either. There was never due process involving charges or trials before incarceration for those detained by T-Force, and the duration of detention varied and had little to do with the importance of the German expert's potential contribution to British knowledge. It was more to do with how long it took the bureaucracy to decide what to do with the person concerned, whether the solution was to release them, hand them over to the denazification courts, or arrange employment with a British firm or university.[74]

T-Force detentions often clashed with the denazification efforts of the BAOR and government of occupation. The latter were initially based more on idealism than pragmatic planning. Early efforts in 1945 were ad hoc and sometimes involved arbitrary decisions which conflicted with the desire to harvest the fruits of Nazi research. For example, it is hard to rationally explain why Ferdinand Porsche was imprisoned for designing tanks, whereas Hellmuth Walter was recruited by the British for designing submarine and aircraft engines.

Eventually, the ACC agreed to a procedure based on a questionnaire about involvement with the Nazis. Five categories of persons were established, including major offenders, offenders, lesser offenders, followers, and exonerated persons. The Americans insisted that every German complete this, but the processing office in Paris required vast human resources and quickly became clogged with papers.

---

[73] Longden, Kindle Edition loc 872
[74] Longden.

The British approach was much more pragmatic. They concentrated on the education system and tried to rehabilitate as many other Germans as possible who could take over responsibility for rebuilding their country including processing the denazification of their neighbors.[75] That said, precisely how the British analyzed the data in order to assign individuals to a category was never made wholly transparent, though some details did emerge as a result of Parliamentary questioning. For example, in the British zone, those who had voted Nazi before 1932 when it was still free and relatively safe not to do so were treated more severely, but the overall lack of transparency meant that the records of individuals wanted for transfer could be whitewashed. There is extensive evidence that this was done by the Americans during Operation Paperclip.[76] Questions remain unanswered regarding the British zone.

While being detained, German experts were interrogated. Memoirs reveal that many T-Force soldiers and assessors struggled with personal feelings; for example, when interrogating those responsible for the V1 and V2 rockets which had, in some cases, devastated their hometowns and killed people they knew. Feelings also ran high after the discovery of the concentration camps.[77] This created the motive for abuse during interrogations. In the days before the Police and Criminal Evidence Act, interviews were not videoed, recorded, or transcribed, so there was ample opportunity for abuse. Questioning could be probing, which is why expert assessors were used, and interrogations were often robust because, while the fighting was still in progress, the Allies needed answers concerning new weapons quickly.[78] It is surely to the credit of the British occupying forces that no evidence has emerged of beatings, torture, or threats against families. On the contrary, families were given rations of food and fuel, and their homes were protected from requisitioning for the duration of interrogations.[79]

From a human resources and information management perspective, very little is known about T-Force interrogations. For instance, it's not clear when interviews were formal or informal, or if the interrogations were conducted by one person or a panel. The British did realize that inducements such as protection from war crimes prosecution and additional rations of food and fuel for the detainees' families would make the Germans more forthcoming, but beyond that, no systematic human resources management planning or techniques were ever applied. That was a lost opportunity.

There were three entirely different sets of circumstances in which German experts came to Britain, and they should not be conflated.

While the war was still in progress, a small number of key figures, including the Uranium Club nuclear physicists (discussed further below), were sent to Britain for interrogation. These men

[75] Alliierten.
[76] Charles Rivers Editors.
[77] Howard; Longden.
[78] Ibid.
[79] Hall.

were given no choice in the matter, and they were flown to Britain under military escort at short notice, detained in secure accommodations on arrival without charge, access to lawyers, or release date, and subjected to electronic surveillance despite not legally being POWs.[80] The circumstances were very similar to the rendition operations carried out in recent years by the CIA against alleged enemies of the United States; the only difference was that the British provided comfortable living conditions and detainees were not physically abused.

The number of men renditioned to the UK in this way is not known. No official register seems to have been kept at the time, and several different agencies, including the British T-Force and the Anglo-American Alsos investigation into German nuclear research, were involved.

Scientists renditioned in late 1944 and early 1945 were in an entirely different situation than those German experts who obtained employment in the UK from 1946-1949, although many of those people had previously been detained and interrogated by T-Force or others. Some were offered employment in the UK by interrogators either because of their immediate usefulness, or to deny them to the Russians. Adolf Busemann, a world leading aerodynamicist, was one example.[81] Many more solicited some form of employment from the British occupation authorities because they saw little future in Germany and preferred to work for the British rather than the Russians. Such letters of application were vetted, and the vast majority appear to have been rejected. Then, as now, British immigration policy was intent on taking only the best who could make a direct contribution to British military capability or economic recovery.[82] The experts who were accepted were not imprisoned on arrival, but most were taken to a holding center in Wimbledon while paperwork was processed. Some were also subject to surveillance by MI5 and restrictions on their movements.[83]

---

[80] Operation Epsilon.
[81] Hall, 125.
[82] Longden.
[83] Brinson, Charmian, and Richard Dove. 2014. *A Matter of Intelligence*. Manchester, England: Manchester University Press, Chapters 17-21.

Busemann

In the case of voluntary recruitment, it is clear that working for the Russians was seen as a last resort, but the British always struggled to compete with the terms offered by the Americans. British policy was also conflicted because alongside recruitment efforts in Britain, there was a deliberate policy, driven by the Treasury from outside BIOS, to reduce the costs of occupation by leaving potential leaders at home in Germany. This drew on practices used to run the British Empire, which depended on a small number of British officials delegating authority to local leaders who could direct their own people to do the work. The British military leaders and Treasury mandarins in occupied Germany quickly came around to the view that rebuilding the country was a higher priority than further transfers.[84]

The well-known case of Volkswagen illustrates this. The machinery at Wolfsburg could have been sent to Britain and the factory managers prosecuted under denazification procedures for employing slave labor, but instead, Major Ivan Hirst and Colonel Charles Radclyffe used the discretion which field officers were given. They were Royal Electrical and Mechanical Engineers (REME) officers and chose not to hand over the site to T-Force. Instead, REME troops helped restart production as early as June 1945, and in doing so created a major competitor for the UK car industry going forward.[85] Representatives of British motor

[84] Knowles, Christopher. 2014. "Germany 1945-49: A Case Study in Post Conflict Reconstruction". Blog. *History and Policy*. http://www.historyandpolicy.org/policy-papers/papers/germany-1945-1949-a-case-study-in-post-conflict-reconstruction.

manufacturers did visit the plant but rejected the opportunity to relocate it, fearing competition. Nobody seems to have foreseen that it would become a global competitor where it was.[86]

The most controversial group of Germans transferred to the UK were those who did not choose to come but were moved against their will so that the Russians could not seize them. A list of around 1,500 such targets was drawn up for T-Force to apprehend in the summer of 1946, and others were detained by MI6 under Operation Dustbin. Rounding them up proved difficult, and there was a sense of desperation in Whitehall. Discussions took place about kidnapping scientists as a last resort.[87]

Upon taking targets into custody, T-Force or MI6 interrogators tried to persuade them to come to the UK. No lists of names have emerged, but it is believed that only around 100 further personnel did enter British service.[88] The reasons for the loss of the remainder are not known. Some may never have been apprehended, while others may have stubbornly rejected the terms and conditions on offer. Others may have been among the German scientists, some of them former Nazi Party or SS members, sent to Australia. This was in defiance of an Australian government ban on the entry of such persons, so it is unclear if these transfers were consensual or forced renditions.[89]

A fourth group of Germans transferred their labor to Britain. The British government rejected the stipulation in the Morgenthau Plan that forced labor should not be used as a form of reparations. In fact, forced labor by German POWs was used extensively to maintain agricultural production in Britain in 1946 and 1947, and they were also made to do building work such as the access road to Wembley Stadium in London. The conditions were not unduly harsh, and German POWs were offered the opportunity to stay on in the UK and become British citizens after their colleagues were repatriated in 1947-1948. Around 20,000 did so and joined the British labor force, albeit at a lower level than the scientists.[90]

British efforts to recruit German experts have to be seen in the context of a global market for German scientific talent, which actually began with the prewar exodus who did not all emigrate to Britain or the US. Then, and in the late 1940s, Britain was competing with emerging universities and governments in places such as Turkey that could offer complete freedom to set up a new department or program according to the scientists' preferences.[91] Michael J. Neufeld

[85] https://www.volkswagen.co.uk/timeline/index?decade=1940&q=&
[86] Hall, 87.
[87] BBC News, 2006
[88] Longden.
[89] Traynor, Ian. 1999. "UK Arranged Transfer of Nazi Scientists to Australia". *The Guardian*, 1999. https://www.theguardian.com/uk/1999/aug/17/iantraynor.
[90] Malpass, Alan. 2017. "What Happened to German Prisoners of War in Britain After Hitler's Defeat". Blog. *The Conversation*. https://theconversation.com/what-happened-to-german-prisoners-of-war-in-britain-after-hitlers-defeat-74859.
[91] Grant, Andrew. 2018. "The Unlikely Haven For 1930S German Scientists". Blog. *Physics Today*. https://physicstoday.scitation.org/do/10.1063/PT.6.4.20180927a/full/.

(2012) has shown that the postwar exodus of aerospace talent also had a global dimension as emerging countries like Argentina, Brazil, Egypt, India, and Spain tried to recruit German experts to kickstart domestic aircraft industries. The existence of this global market for talent meant that German scientists and engineers soon realized they could negotiate. Four things were uppermost in their minds: facilities and academic freedom to continue their work; assistance, including relocation for their families; immunity from war crimes prosecutions; and competitive salaries and working conditions. The Russians were willing to promise all four and equally willing to break those promises, as Manfred von Ardenne, an eminent nuclear physicist and radio and TV pioneer, discovered to his cost. Manfred von Ardenne, a cyclotron designer, and his wife recounted, "With relatively light hearts, we left the children and everything else behind in Lichterfeld because we had gone for a two-week trip to the Soviet Union 'only to conclude a contract.' Those two weeks turned into ten years." [92] Once in Russia, most of the scientists received no release to return to their homes in Germany for 10 years, with many returns permitted in 1955. Even those few scientists actually interned by the Western Allies, by contrast, typically found themselves back in Germany (if they did not wish to remain in a different country) by 1948.

Pay and the welfare of families played a big role in the destination of German experts. After the success of Operation Backfire to assemble and test fire V2 rockets in late 1945 at Cuxhaven, the Americans succeeded in recruiting all but a few dozen of the hundreds of German scientists and technicians who had worked under allied military supervision. They did it by offering superior terms and conditions, and including family relocation in job offers. This meant the Americans gained the benefit of learning from the Germans' mistakes and thus quickly sped up their own ballistic missile development program.[93] The British did not learn and continued to pay submarket rates to their detained technicians writing reports at Rheinmetall-Borsig until 1948. Not surprisingly, they too opted not to transfer to Britain.[94]

The simple fact is that the British authorities were not very good at persuasion because they were very slow to realize that they were dealing with a human resources management issue, namely how to compete in a global market for talent. Admittedly, there was an Enemy Personnel Exploitation Section (EPES), set up on May 1, 1945 under the auspices of FIAT, which had both British and American sections. It accumulated a card index of about 18,000 names and was used by military and civilian investigation teams to identify the people they needed to interrogate or attempt to recruit in particular specialties.[95] Intelligence skills were used to identify and locate the experts, but beyond that, however, EPES seems to have been nothing more than a clerical exercise. There is no evidence that it developed coherent human resources policies to attract experts to work for Britain rather than a rival power. Furthermore, when policy changes did

---

[92] https://en.wikipedia.org/wiki/Manfred_von_Ardenne
[93] Hall, 98.
[94] Ibid., 112
[95] Ibid., 110

occur, they were always reactive rather than proactive.

There were actually three phases of British recruitment: the Deputy Chiefs of Staff (DCOS) scheme; the Darwin Panel; and "Exclusive exploitation." The first two schemes meant that German scientists could only be recruited by British state agencies for the benefit of national defense or an entire industry, that meant the state owned their IP. Exclusive exploitation, which was not agreed to until mid-1947, meant that individual private sector firms could contract with scientists and own the intellectual property rights on their work. All three phases were bureaucratic in operation, so many experts were lost to delays.

British recruitment policies were also slow and reactive when it came to guarantees of permanent settlement, which obviously discouraged experts who were concerned about the continuity of their children's education.[96]

The Impact of the British Efforts

Despite their deficiencies, the scale of British transfers from Germany to the UK after World War II was still huge. Estimates of the numbers involved have increased dramatically in recent years, but precise quantification remains hazardous because no records were kept of the early stages of the operation, and some files remain closed.

CIOS sent out 2,197 personnel and visited 3,377 locations even before hostilities ceased.[97] The pace of activity increased markedly after Germany's surrender, and by the end of 1946, 6,590 tons of equipment had been shipped back to Britain and a further 11,182 tons were in storage awaiting transport.[98] In the last days of T-Force operations, in mid-1947, T-Force was handling the logistics for an average of 200 visits a month by teams from the British private sector.[99] As a result of those visits, around 70,000 patents based on German research had been filed with the British patent office by the end of 1947.[100]

The most serious gap in knowledge is the scale and nature of personnel transfers. The published reports were based in part on the interrogation of experts but do not contain information on their subsequent fate. The EPES card index contained around 18,000 names but did not identify which ones were renditioned to the UK or recruited voluntarily. There is no database of names for either category, but the most thorough study puts the number at just under 1,000. That figure is much greater than is generally realized and fairly close to the recruitment levels of the United States (but well short of the 1,600 experts taken to Russia through Operation Osoaviakhim).[101] This estimate does not include the POWs or the prewar refugees who stayed on

---

[96] Hall, Chapter 6.

[97] Ibid. 57.

[98] Ibid. 87

[99] Ibid. p89

[100] Ibid. p174

[101] Glatt, Carl, Reparations and the Transfer of Scientific and Industrial Technology from Germany: A Case Study of

in Britain.

Once an investigation had been completed, the findings were written up, and tis could take two forms. The British forced German experts to write academic papers and reports for the benefit of their captors. The British, for example, detained about 150 experts from a variety of disciplines at the Rheinmetall-Borsig Factory until 1948, where they were writing such papers.[102] The other common method was reports based on interviews and seized documents written by T-Force assessors and published by BIOS.

These reports were the main measure the British government used at the time to monitor the scale and impact of the British transfer policy. However, modern sources disagree about the precise number. Knowles (2010) estimates the total at 1,400, but Hall (2019) thinks 3,000 is more likely. including those of a military nature which are still secret.[103]

By early 1946, an increasingly sophisticated system developed to disseminate BIOS reports which concerned civilian industrial processes to potential beneficiaries in British industry. The Board of Trade organized an exhibition in London in December 1946 that subsequently toured the country, and almost two million copies of the various reports were sold or given to business leaders and public libraries.[104] Representatives of individual firms were also enabled to visit factories in Germany under T-Force supervision and order machinery to be delivered to their UK premises to replace obsolete or worn out items.[105]

Due the enormous range of technologies transferred, it is impossible to cover them all, but the British government understandably attached higher priority to some of them.

Stemming from the belief in German technical superiority and fear of wonder weapons, one of the highest priorities given to T-Force was the capture of the leading scientists researching the German nuclear weapons program, known as *Uranprojekt* ("Uranium Club"). Churchill believed the Germans had a two-year lead in nuclear technology and might develop the capability to explode a dirty bomb over London.[106] Commandoes and the RAF disabled the Germans' heavy water plant in Norway, but as Germany collapsed, the British still had no knowledge of how much had survived. They feared that the technology could still be in the hands of Nazi fanatics intending to carry out werewolf attacks.[107]

the roots of British Industrial Policy and of Aspects of British Occupation Policy in Germany between Post-World War II Reconstruction and the Korean War, PhD dissertation, European University institute, Florence (1994) cited by Hall. 2019. Op cit. Chapter 6.

[102] Vella, Heidi. 2016. "How Nazis Ended Up Working for The Allies After World War II". Blog. *Engineering and Technology*. https://eandt.theiet.org/content/articles/2016/12/how-nazis-ended-up-working-for-the-allies-after-wwii/; Hall, 111.

[103] Knowles, Christopher. 2010. "How Much Was T-Force Worth to The British Economy?". Blog. *How It Really Was*. https://howitreallywas.typepad.com/how_it_really_was/t-force/.

[104] Hall, 88.

[105] Longden.

[106] Lewis, Damien. 2016. *Hunting Hitler's Nukes*. Quercus.

These fears led to Operation Epsilon. Between May 1 and June 30, 1945, T-Force captured a huge number of documents and 10 German nuclear scientists as part of the Anglo-American Alsos Mission. All 10 were renditioned to Britain and interned in a bugged country house, Farm Hall, Godmanchester near Cambridge. The Farm Hall prisoners were not allowed to take their families with them, and the intelligence reports make it clear that this caused anxiety and made the scientists less cooperative; a lesson which was learned during later detentions and interrogations when families were looked after.[108]

The Uranium Club had distinguished academic records, but, to the surprise of the British, the transcripts of their conversations obtained by MI5 revealed that the Germans were still facing some of the technical obstacles the British and Americans had broken through around 1940.[109] Having concluded that the Uranium Club scientists were of little value, the British released them in December 1945. All of them returned to Germany, but the subsequent career of Heisenberg reveals what might have been. He resumed his academic career and re-established the Max Planck Institute for Physics at Gottingen. Britain did not lose his expertise entirely, as he was a visiting Professor at Cambridge and St Andrews Universities in the 1940s and 1950s, but had human resources tools been employed, such as relocating his family to the UK and finding him a tenured university post, his prodigious talents might have been utilized to establish a British equivalent of the Max Planck Institute in the 1950s and 1960s.

The Fedden Mission, led by Sir Roy Fedden, was one of the earliest attempts to exploit German technological developments to benefit an entire British industry, civil as well as military. Much of the 2,000 tons of equipment seized and the knowledge gleaned ended up at the newly founded College of Aeronautics at Cranfield.[110] However, Fedden came to believe that most of the potential benefits of transfers had again been lost.[111]

German jet engine research had focused on axial flow engines. These were much slimmer than British designs, which used centrifugal compressors, but examples transferred from BMW and Jumo proved to be of inferior quality because they had been rushed into production with insufficient development and because Germany lacked access to the special metals required to prevent turbine blade fractures and to withstand extreme heat.[112] Axial flow technology was incorporated in the De Havilland Vampire and Comet airliner, among others, with the engines buried in the wing roots, but the British had to start again to operationalize the concept. In other words, the popular belief that German technology ushered in the jet age in Britain is unfounded.

---

[107] Ibid.

[108] Operation Epsilon.

[109] Bernstein, Jeremy. 2001. *Hitler's Uranium Club: The Secret recordings at Farm Hall* (2nd ed.). New York: Springer-Verlag.

[110] Hall, 98.

[111] Coneybeare.

[112] Uziel, Daniel. 2019. "Jet Engine Development in Germany - TFOT". *TFOT*. https://thefutureofthings.com/3809-jet-engine-development-in-germany/.

What German experts did do was usher in the age of subsonic and supersonic flight in Britain through their advances in aerodynamics, particularly swept wings and delta wings. A second more organized mission followed Fedden's in November 1946 and recovered test rigs, a wind tunnel, and huge quantities of documentation from Völkenrode and AVA, Reyershausen.[113] Analysis of these transfers resulted in Air Ministry Specification B35/46 issued in 1946 which yielded the nuclear capable V Bombers that enabled Britain to preserve the illusion of being a world power through the 1950s and 1960s.[114] Swept wings were also incorporated into the prestigious but ill-fated De Havilland Comet and the hugely successful Vickers Viscount civil airliners, while tailless delta wings crossed over into civil aviation in the Concorde. However, the British made only limited use of German advances in rocketry and space exploration. The Americans had obtained most of the best brains in this field, especially von Braun and his team, and attempting to compete proved too costly.

British concerns that the Germans had superior nuclear weapons technology proved to be unfounded, but with radar the British began the war believing that they had a major advantage that turned out to be illusory. British radar was vital in the Battle of Britain, but it was primarily defensive, in line with the pacifist sentiment arising from World War I. The Germans, on the other hand, focused on offensive radar, particularly direction-finding systems which could guide bombers to their targets.[115] The Bruneval Raid carried out by the Allies in February 1942 arose from the need to understand how this *Wurzberg* radar worked, and the documents captured encouraged the expansion of later T-Force operations. However, they did not stop the Germans from further developing the principle, so near the end of the war T-Force operations recovered a huge range of experimental techniques for guiding anti-aircraft fire, naval gunnery, torpedoes, and bombs dropped from aircraft.[116] Unlike many of the more famous German "wonder weapons," most of this was incremental research in specialist areas such as gyroscopes. It attracted little attention then or since, but it had a profound effect on the development of all manner of military and civilian applications.

Both sides had stockpiles of gases and chemical weapons during World War II, but neither chose to use them. Consequently, chemical weapons were low on the list of CIOS and T-Force priorities until investigators stumbled on a completely new class of gases in the spring of 1945:

---

[113] Hall, 100.

[114] *Wynn, Humphrey. 1997. RAF Strategic Nuclear Deterrent Forces, Their Origins, Roles and Deployment, 1946–1969. A Documentary History.* London: HMSO.

[115] Clark, Gregory C. 2010. "Deflating British Radar Myths of World War II — Articles | 1939 | 1940 | History | Pre-War". *Spitfiresite.Com.* http://spitfiresite.com/2010/04/deflating-british-radar-myths-of-world-war-ii.html/6.

[116] Longden.

nerve agents developed by I.G. Farben and readied for delivery in artillery shells. Two main types were identified - tabun and sarin samples – and they were captured by T-Force and sent to the Chemical Defence Experimental Establishment (CDEE) at Porton Down for investigation.[117]

Sarin became a mainstay of Britain's Cold War deterrence, and a huge amount of highly controversial research was carried out into its effects and possible countermeasures through the 1950s and 1960s.[118] Questions remain unanswered about the possible role of research done by German doctors on concentration camp victims in these experiments. The memoirs of T-Force survivors speak of seeing an archive of photographs of the effects of chemical weapons on concentration camp victims, but if they existed, they are missing.[119] It is possible that they were secretly utilized in British research, most likely as an indicator of what data existed and what experiments did not need to be repeated again.

Britain did recruit some German chemists, but, amidst continuing secrecy and obfuscation by modern governments, it is impossible to be certain whether they did or did not work on sarin experiments at Porton Down.[120] Meanwhile, it is known that all four of the inventors of sarin were released from American war crimes prisons in the early 1950s and resumed their careers in the international chemical industry, including advising British companies.[121]

There is a tendency to assume that the sheer scale of German technology and personnel transferred to Britain must have fundamentally changed British industry. However, academic historians disagree for several reasons. The first concerns concentration, because unlike the Americans and Russians, the British did not concentrate their German experts in national prestige projects such as nuclear weapons or space exploration. Moreover, there was no coherent government policy to concentrate German expertise in "sunrise industries" such as television or petrochemicals. Individual companies such as Pye and Courtaulds did recruit Germans, but there was no human resources policy to support them.[122] There is no definitive list of organizations that received either material assets or personnel from Nazi Germany, and there is a dearth of case studies at the firm or individual level, but it seems likely that German knowledge was spread among hundreds of firms, military establishments, and universities.

A second issue concerned delays in granting access to German resources. It was not until 1946 that civilian firms were allowed access to sites under the control of T-Force. After that, extensive transfers of IP and equipment did take place, but transfers of personnel had to wait even longer until the "Exclusive exploitation" scheme was approved in mid-1947. By then, many industries

---

[117] Longden, Kindle Ed 318ff

[118] Schmidt, Ulf. 2006. "Cold War at Porton Down: Informed Consent in Britain's Biological and Chemical Warfare Experiments". *Cambridge Quarterly of Healthcare Ethics* 15 (1): 366-380.

[119] Longden.

[120] Hall, Chapter 6.

[121] Mining Awareness. 2014. "SARIN Nerve Gas, I.G. Farben, and the Nazis". *Mining Awareness +*. https://miningawareness.wordpress.com/2014/07/03/sarin-nerve-gas-i-g-farben-and-the-nazis/.

[122] Hall.

were well on the way to recovery independently. In any case, BIOS reports were shared with Britain's allies, and even the Russians were allowed to buy them, so any competitive advantage gained by British firms was short lived.[123]

A third issue concerns what was learned. While there was a serious effort to disseminate transferred knowledge as widely as possible among British firms, that does not mean the information was actually read or acted upon. Furthermore, most of the reports concerned machinery and production processes. Some British firms did replace obsolete or worn out machinery, but replacing machines does not equal changes in human capital management or working practices. Extensive German use of slave labor meant they had nothing to teach the British on this point.

The fourth issue concerns the role of the trade unions. It is an open question whether the parsimonious attitude of the British authorities to incentivize German experts and thus limit their number was the result of pressure from trade unions on the Labour government. Wrigley (1997) noted there were isolated instances of opposition to the employment of German experts, and these seem to have been motivated by a mixture of ideological hatred of Nazis, fear of competition driving down wages, and an unwillingness to embrace new ideas and new ways of working.[124] This was following precedent. The unions forced the government to dismiss most women wartime workers and reimpose demarcation and other restrictive practices after 1918 in order to preserve wages and employment for their members. Management and politicians acquiesced in this, and productivity growth, profitability, and investment remained generally sluggish in the interwar period. The same may have happened after 1945, leading to German expertise being underutilized.[125]

Yet another limitation of transfers from Germany was that they did not benefit the infrastructure on which British companies relied to operate efficiently. Almost all of Germany's infrastructure, ports, roads, railways, power stations, and the like were destroyed during the war. T-Force secured what was left but handed it over to the British government of occupation rather than transferring it. Thus, there is no record of any of the designers of the German autobahns, for example, being renditioned or recruited, and Britain did not get an equivalent, the M1, until 1959. Meanwhile, British infrastructure remained worn out and underinvested in the postwar period despite nationalization.[126] This reduced the effect of technological transfers.

As explained by Knowles (2010), trying to come up with a financial value for what the British transferred back from Germany is futile. The contemporary official estimates in the National Archives at Kew are worthless.[127] No inventories were kept until the beginning of 1946, and the

---

[123] Hall.

[124] Wrigley, Chris. 1997. *British Trade Unions*. Manchester: Manchester Univ. Press.

[125] Ibid.

[126] Hennessey.

[127] Knowles, Christopher. 2010. "How Much Was T-Force Worth to The British Economy?". Blog. *How It Really*

rules formulated by IARA after that created a strong incentive to falsify the figures by misclassifying reparations as booty to avoid its inclusion in Britain's national quota. Figures produced by T-Force survivors such as Howard (2010) of £2 billion at today's values sound impressive but are nothing more than guesstimates and still fall far short of the costs of the British zone of occupation between 1945 and 1954.

The main issue is that the most valuable transfers to Britain were intangible assets in the form of IP and knowledge, and even in modern accounting, the basis of valuation for such intangibles is problematic. So much of the value of intangible assets comes not from possession but from the effectiveness of exploitation. The other issue is how to put a figure on opportunity savings, such as research Britain did not need to repeat, for example in aerodynamics and the benefits of denying IP to the Russians and Western competitors. Rather than arguing about the value that transfers did bring to the British economy, it is more important to recognize that the value could have been much higher with the application of better human resources management techniques and better economic planning.

The unplanned dispersal of German expertise across British industry and academia dissipated the economic impact, but it did have social benefits. It meant that there were no concentrations of Germans in particular locations where they could have caused resentment, and large numbers of educated Britons met and worked with individual Germans who were broadly supportive of the UK and its values. The effect of this on British openness to the rehabilitation of Germany can be seen in contemporary opinion polls regarding Germany and the German people, which showed a rapid shift in the late 1940s and early 1950s.[128]

Conversely, the relative humanity of policies in the British zone of occupation made many Germans favorably disposed to the British. Troops ignored the fraternization ban imposed in an attempt to learn the lessons of Versailles, and it had been abandoned by the end of 1945 except for interracial marriage.[129] British transfer policies ignored intellectual property rights and imposed widespread detentions and interrogations, but the British used unethical methods of coercion and kidnapping far less than the Russians. More importantly, they brought stability and the restoration of infrastructure. In addition, the British had a policy of putting Germans back to work to assist their own recovery under British supervision. It was motivated primarily by the desire to cut costs, but it had the effect of reducing the rigors of denazification in the British zone, creating employment, and enabling British and Germans to learn to work together.[130] Taken together, the social effect of British transfer policies was that it broke down racial

---

Was. https://howitreallywas.typepad.com/how_it_really_was/t-force/.

[128] Judt.

[129] Knowles, Christopher. 2009. "Field Marshal Montgomery and the Fraternisation Ban". Blog. *How It Really Was*. https://howitreallywas.typepad.com/how_it_really_was/2009/03/fieldmarshal-montgomery-and-the-fraternisation-ban.html.

[130] Knowles. 2014.

stereotypes of all Germans as Nazis and made future European integration feasible.

As all of this suggests, political leaders who have to deal with the end of 21st century wars can look to what happened in 1945 for certain lessons. For example, there has to be a sense of justice, and that justice should not be compromised by cynical economic advantage for the victors. In that manner, the desire for reparations has to be balanced with the need to avoid having the defeated nations become a source of economic and social instability.

Perhaps most importantly, given the state of European politics today, displaced populations should be viewed as pools of talent that can be utilized to enhance the global economy, not as threats.

Online Resources

Other World War II titles by Charles River Editors

Further Reading

Allied Control Council. 1946. "Allied Control Authority Germany, Enactments and Approved Papers, 9 Volumes (Berlin, 1946–1948), Covering the Period 1945–1948". Washington: United States Government.

Alliierten Museum. 2019. "Denazification | Alliiertenmuseum Berlin". *Alliiertenmuseum.De*. http://www.alliiertenmuseum.de/en/topics/denazification.html.

Avalon Project. 2008. "The Avalon Project: Yalta (Crimea) Conference". *Avalon.Law.Yale.Edu*. https://avalon.law.yale.edu/wwii/yalta.asp.

BBC News. 2006. "BBC NEWS | UK | UK 'Fears' Over German Scientists". *News.Bbc.Co.Uk*. http://news.bbc.co.uk/1/hi/uk/4862054.stm.

Beckert, Helen. 2016. "The Effects of Denazification on Education in West Germany". Bachelors, Murray.

Bernstein, Jeremy. 2001. *Hitler's Uranium Club: The Secret recordings at Farm Hall* (2nd ed.). New York: Springer-Verlag.

Brinson, Charmian, and Richard Dove. 2014. *A Matter of Intelligence*. Manchester, England: Manchester University Press.

Cabinet Office. 2019. "WWII British War Cabinet Notebooks". *Paperlessarchives.Com*. Accessed June 24. http://paperlessarchives.com/wwii_british_war_cabinet_.html.

Charles River Editors. 2019. *Operation Paperclip: The History of the Secret Program to Bring*

Christopher, John. 2013. *The Race for Hitler's X-Planes*. London: Trafalgar Square Publishing.

Clark, Gregory C. 2010. "Deflating British Radar Myths of World War II — Articles | 1939 | 1940 | History | Prewar". *Spitfiresite.Com*. http://spitfiresite.com/2010/04/deflating-british-radar-myths-of-world-war-ii.html/6.

Cobain, Ian. 2007. "How T-Force Abducted Germany's Best Brains for Britain". *The Guardian*, 2007. https://www.theguardian.com/science/2007/aug/29/sciencenews.secondworldwar.

Coneybeare, John. 2011. "Sir Roy Fedden (1885-1973)". Blog. *Engineer's Walk*. http://www.engineerswalk.co.uk/rf_walk.html.

Farquharson, John. 1997. "Governed or Exploited? The British Acquisition of German Technology, 1945-48". *Journal of Contemporary History* 32 (1): 23-42. doi:10.1177/002200949703200103.

Foreign and Commonwealth Office. 1998. "British Policy Towards Enemy Property During and After the Second World War". History Notes. London.

Grant, Andrew. 2018. "The Unlikely Haven for 1930s German Scientists". Blog. *Physics Today*. https://physicstoday.scitation.org/do/10.1063/PT.6.4.20180927a/full/.

Hall, Charlie. 2019. *British Exploitation of German Science and Technology, 1943-1949*. Abingdon: Routledge.

Harrod, Roy. 2003. *The Life of John Maynard Keynes*. Houndmills, UK: Palgrave Macmillan.

Hennessy, Peter. 1992. *Never Again*. London: J. Cape.

Howard, Michael. 2010. *Otherwise Occupied*. Tiverton, Devon: Old Street.

IARA. 2019. "Inter-Allied Reparation Agency: Papers of UK Delegation | The National Archives". *Discovery.Nationalarchives.Gov.Uk*. https://discovery.nationalarchives.gov.uk/details/r/C14031.

JCS1067. 2008. "Avalon Project – Directive to Commander-In-Chief of United States Forces of Occupation Regarding the Military Government of Germany; April 1945". *Avalon.Law.Yale.Edu*. https://avalon.law.yale.edu/wwii/ger02.asp.

Jewish Virtual Library. 2019. "The Ethics of Using Medical Data from Nazi Experiments". *Jewishvirtuallibrary.Org*. https://www.jewishvirtuallibrary.org/the-ethics-of-using-medical-data-from-nazi-experiments.

Judt, Tony. 2010. *Post War: A History of Europe Since 1945*. Vintage.

Knowles, Christopher. 2009. "Field Marshal Montgomery and the Fraternisation Ban". Blog. *How It Really Was*. https://howitreallywas.typepad.com/how_it_really_was/2009/03/fieldmarshal-montgomery-and-the-fraternisation-ban.html.

Knowles, Christopher. 2010. "How Much Was T-Force Worth to The British Economy?". Blog. *How It Really Was*. https://howitreallywas.typepad.com/how_it_really_was/t-force/.

Knowles, Christopher. 2014. "Germany 1945-49: A Case Study in Post Conflict Reconstruction". Blog. *History and Policy*. http://www.historyandpolicy.org/policy-papers/papers/germany-1945-1949-a-case-study-in-post-conflict-reconstruction.

Lewis, Damien. 2016. *Hunting Hitler's Nukes*. Quercus.

Longden, Sean. 2009. *T-Force: The Race for Nazi War Secrets, 1945*. Constable & Robinson.

Macmillan, Margaret Olwen. 2003. *Six Months That Changed the World*. Prince Frederick, Md.: Recorded Books.

Malpass, Alan. 2017. "What Happened to German Prisoners of War in Britain After Hitler's Defeat". Blog. *The Conversation*. https://theconversation.com/what-happened-to-german-prisoners-of-war-in-britain-after-hitlers-defeat-74859.

Mining Awareness. 2014. "SARIN Nerve Gas, I.G. Farben, and the Nazis". *Mining Awareness +*. https://miningawareness.wordpress.com/2014/07/03/sarin-nerve-gas-i-g-farben-and-the-nazis/.

Morgenthau, Henry. 1944. "Suggested Post Surrender Program for Germany". *Waybackmachine*. https://web.archive.org/web/20130531235410/http://docs.fdrlibrary.marist.edu/psf/box31/t297a01.htm.

Naimark, Norman (1995). *The Russians in Germany*. Harvard University Press

Neufeld, Michael J. 2012. "The Nazi Aerospace Exodus: Towards A Global, Transnational History". *History and Technology* 28 (1): 49-67. doi:10.1080/07341512.2012.662338.

The Nobel Institute. 2019. "The Nobel Prize in Physics 1932". *Nobelprize.Org*. Accessed June 25. https://www.nobelprize.org/prizes/physics/1932/heisenberg/biographical/.

Operation Epsilon. 2019. "World War II: Operation EPSILON Detention of German Nuclear Scientists British Intelligence Files". *Paperlessarchives.Com*. http://paperlessarchives.com/wwii-operation-epsilon.html.

Redmond, Caroline. 2019. "The Nuremberg Trials: When the World Tried to Bring the Nazis To Justice and Failed". Blog. *All That's Interesting*. https://allthatsinteresting.com/nuremberg-trials.

Schmidt, Ulf. 2006. "Cold War at Porton Down: Informed Consent in Britain's Biological and Chemical Warfare Experiments". *Cambridge Quarterly of Healthcare Ethics* 15 (1): 366-380.

Taylor, Frederick. 2011. *Exorcising Hitler: The Occupation and Denazification of Germany*. Bloomsbury Publishing.

Traynor, Ian. 1999. "UK Arranged Transfer of Nazi Scientists to Australia". *The Guardian*, 1999. https://www.theguardian.com/uk/1999/aug/17/iantraynor.

Uziel, Daniel. 2019. "Jet Engine Development in Germany - TFOT". *TFOT*. https://thefutureofthings.com/3809-jet-engine-development-in-germany/.

Walters, Guy. 2015. "The Real Hero in The Grylls Family". *The Daily Mail*, 2015. https://www.dailymail.co.uk/news/article-3128846/Bear-Grylls-grandfather-Ted-revealed-commander-elite-unit-tracked-Nazi-secrets.html.

Wheeler Bennett, John. 1954. *The Nemesis of Power, The German Army in Politics, 1918-1945*. 1st ed. London: Macmillan.

Wrigley, Chris. 1997. *British Trade Unions*. Manchester: Manchester Univ. Press.

Wynn, Humphrey. 1997. *RAF Strategic Nuclear Deterrent Forces, Their Origins, Roles and Deployment, 1946–1969. A Documentary History*. London: HMSO.

Free Books by Charles River Editors

We have brand new titles available for free most days of the week. To see which of our titles are currently free, click on this link.

Discounted Books by Charles River Editors

We have titles at a discount price of just 99 cents everyday. To see which of our titles are currently 99 cents, click on this link.

Made in the USA
Monee, IL
10 August 2023